making
curtains
& blinds

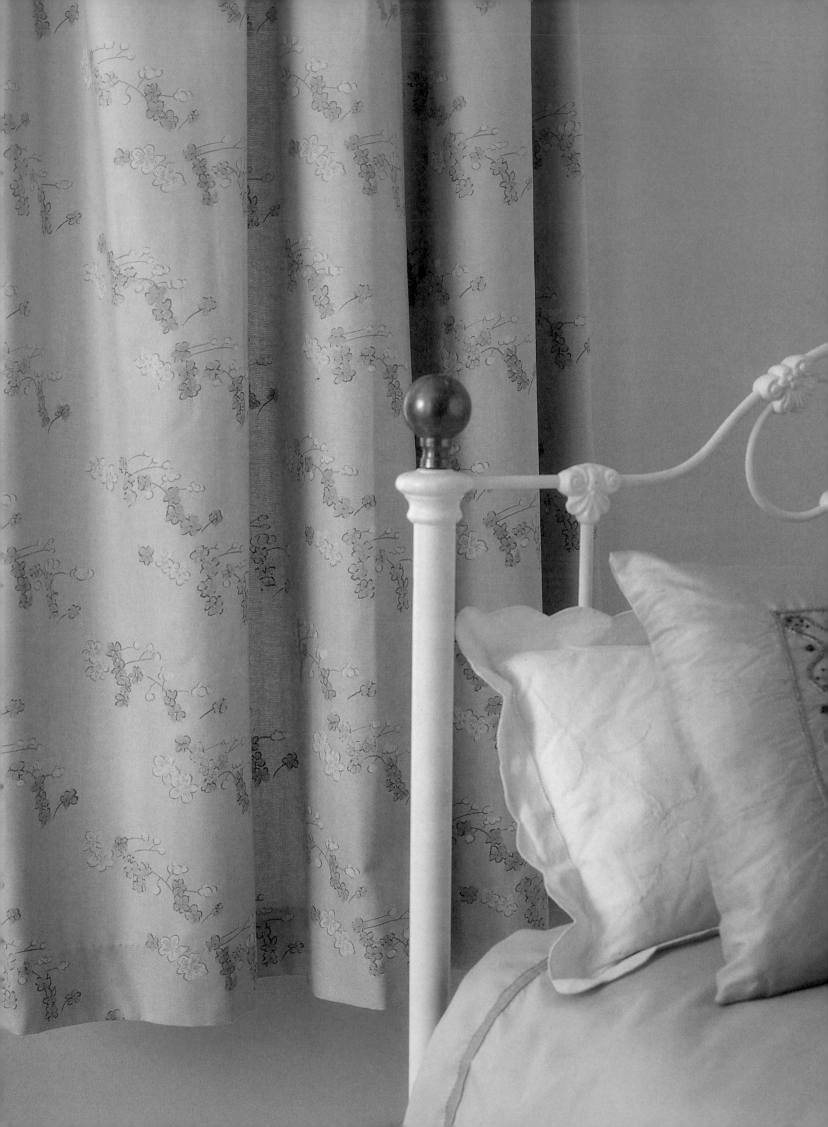

making
curtains
& blinds
dorothy wood

stylish window treatments for every room

southwater

This edition is published by Southwater

Southwater is an imprint of
Anness Publishing Limited
Hermes House
88–89 Blackfriars Road
London
SE1 8HA
tel. 020 7401 2077
fax 020 7633 9499

Distributed in the UK by
The Manning Partnership
251–253 London Road East
Batheaston
Bath BA1 7RL
tel. 01225 852 727
fax 01225 852 852

Published in the USA by
Anness Publishing Inc.
27 West 20th Street
Suite 504
New York
NY 10011
fax 212 807 6813

Distributed in Australia by
Sandstone Publishing
Unit 1, 360 Norton Street
Leichhardt
New South Wales 2040
tel. 02 9560 7888
fax 02 9560 7488

10 9 8 7 6 5 4 3 2

Publisher **Joanna Lorenz**
Managing Editor **Judith Simons**
Project Editor **Simona Hill**
Photographer **Paul Bricknell**
Step-by-step Photographer **Rodney Forte**
Stylist **Juliana Leite Goad**
Designer **Lisa Tai**
Production Controller **Don Campaniello**

Previously published as part of a larger compendium,
The Practical Encyclopedia of Soft Furnishings.

Anness Publishing Ltd and the author would like to
thank Pat Smith of Classic Drapes tel: 0115 945 2210 for
the curtains and blinds.

Thanks to the following organizations and individuals who
generously loaned images for inclusion in this book:
KA International p6 above, p8 above left and below left.
Malabar p14.
prêt à vivre p6 below, p7 right and p12.
Romo p18, p82 top and p83.
Zoffany p35.
Elizabeth Whiting Associates p20.
IPC Magazines p8 below, p18.

contents

introduction

Regardless of size, a window is more often than not the focal point of a room and the way it is covered is an important element in interior decoration. Curtains or blinds immediately give a room a "lived-in" look, and different styles can change the appearance and mood of a room dramatically. It is essential to take into consideration the proportions of the window and to choose a treatment that not only suits your personal taste but also the proportions of the window and its shape in relation to the room. Choose fabric for curtains and blinds carefully; not only will you live with them for a long time, they also need to be the correct weight, and the style needs to suit the purpose of the room they are in.

right Luxurious interlined silk curtains have been made extra long to pool on to the floor. They are not designed to be closed except on cold, winter nights as the blind can be lowered to screen the light.

above left Sheer unlined curtains in a pretty striped floral pattern give a lovely summery feel to this light, airy room. The pelmet board has been covered in a strip of fabric, softened with deep, inverted box pleats at each end.

below left Unusual fabrics with bold patterns can be used successfully on simple blinds.

Professionally made curtains and blinds can be prohibitively expensive but much of this cost is in labour charges so it is well worth making them yourself. Some of the skills required are similar to dressmaking, but it is easier to make curtains and blinds as the seams are usually straight. This book starts with simple, unlined curtains, describes how to line and interline curtains, and progresses to impressive swags and tails. It finishes with a selection of blinds that are easy to make.

As well as the immense satisfaction of creating beautiful, practical window treatments, there is tremendous pleasure to be gained from choosing the best style of curtains or blinds and finding the ideal colour and pattern of fabric. There is so much choice available today that it may seem daunting even before you start but, by selecting the reasons for covering a window, you can begin to narrow the choice. Curtains and blinds have several purposes: they can provide privacy, screen an unattractive view, block out the light or provide insulation from noise and cold. The curtain or blind on a bedroom window, for example, needs to provide privacy and block out the light in the early morning – other rooms in the house will have quite different needs.

As each room in the house has a specific function it should be approached separately. Unless you are starting completely from scratch in a new house, the existing furnishings should be taken into

consideration. The first decision you have to make is the kind of atmosphere or visual impact you want to achieve. Looking through books and magazines will give you ideas and browsing through furnishing fabric departments will bring you up to date with current trends and colours. Even if you are aiming for a contemporary look, there is a wide variety of styles, such as Oriental, folk art, minimalist or ethnic to choose from.

The style you choose will depend on the size and shape of the window or windows in relation to the room, and should reflect the style of your furnishings and the period the house was built. The window treatment for a Georgian town house with high ceilings and very tall windows will be quite different from a modern house with low ceilings and short windows. Most windows look best if the curtains reach the floor, but proportion is very important and the scale of the window treatment should match the room. Tall

right Heavy striped ticking curtains are used as a room divider to hide the kitchen area in this holiday home.
below A white sheer curtain screens the window, and a coloured voile allows the light to filter through gently.
below left Floral prints look equally good in the town or country. They frame the view from these room-length windows beautifully.
above left The warm-coloured fabric behind this panel of cupboards softens the look of the bathroom and makes it look less clinical.

windows look more in proportion with elegant swags and tails or a deep valance with tie-backs to balance their height. In small country cottages, swags and tails would completely overwhelm the room. Traditional cottages often have bays or deeply recessed windows, which suit a window treatment that reaches the windowsill or at most the radiator.

Curtains and blinds are not only restricted to windows. They can also be used for screens and partitions in certain situations. Perhaps it is difficult to fit a door, or you may want to hang a large curtain across a room to hide the cooking area in a kitchen/diner for a dinner party or special occasion.

Curtains and blinds also make excellent "doors" for wardrobes (closets) or shelf units. The fabric softens the harsh lines of woodwork, hides any clutter and keeps the dust away. Lightweight, softly gathered sheer fabrics can be fitted behind clear panels in wardrobe doors. The fabric screens the contents and gives a warmer look especially if there are several doors in the room.

Whatever you decide to make, there will be a similar project in this book. Read through the technical section before you begin and make sure you have all the equipment to help you complete the project as easily as possible.

curtain fittings

Curtains can be hung from a wide range of tracks and poles and the type that you choose will depend on the style of the room, the weight of the fabric used to make the curtain and the finished appearance you want to achieve. Most curtains can be fitted from either a curtain track or a pole. If there is no valance or pelmet, a pole is the more attractive option, since poles are frequently decorative features in their own right. Curtain tracks can be fitted with a valance rail or attached to the underside of a pelmet board. Always ensure that you use the correct type of hook to suit the curtain fitting and heading tape chosen.

Brass track

This high-quality traditional rail is ideal for conservatories because it can withstand high temperatures without distorting. It has a certain unique design appeal in ultra-modern houses and the metal rollers run very smoothly.

Brass café rod

This beautiful brass rod is too elegant to cover. It can be used with a self-heading curtain but looks particularly elegant when the curtain is hung from brass rings.

Contemporary curtain pole

The finials on this retro-look curtain pole are available in a range of shapes and colours to suit your decor. You can choose from many different poles and fit matching tie-backs to create a distinctive and individual look for your room.

Wrought iron pole

Wrought iron poles make a distinct design statement in the home. These poles are less heavy than traditional wrought iron and are suitable for light- to medium-weight fabrics. Several different finials are available to suit your particular decor.

Wooden pole

Wooden poles are normally supplied with matching curtain rings. They are available in a variety of different wood and decorative paint finishes, and with a choice of carved finials.

Brass curtain clips

Curtain clips are a modern alternative to traditional curtain hooks. They do away with curtain tapes and are ideal for simple curtains. Curtain clips are spaced evenly along the top of the curtain (in the same way as bulldog clips grip paper), and the hoop at the top of the grip slides on to the pole.

Hold-backs

Hold-backs are used to hold the curtain away from the window. With some, the curtain is simply draped over the pole and held in place by the decorative disc, and with others a tie-back is used.

Net wire

This steel wire with a plastic coating can be cut to length and fitted using hooks and eyes. It is suitable for sheer or lightweight fabrics with a simple self-heading.

Net track

This lightweight, extendible track is suitable for sheer and lightweight fabrics. Some types can be fitted to the window with hooks or fittings. Others have adhesive pads for use with plastic frame windows.

Valance track

This standard valance track is fitted behind the curtain rail fittings and can be bent to fit a bay window. It is strong enough to be used for all weights of valance.

Cord track

Cord tracks are pre-corded to allow easy access for opening and closing curtains without touching them. This type is suitable for straight runs with medium-weight curtains.

PVC curtain track

This is a basic, general-purpose curtain track, which is easy to fit and to remove if you are decorating the room. It is suitable for mediumweight curtains and can be bent into shape.

Curtain hooks

Curtain hooks are made to fit particular curtain tracks. The end hooks have a screw to keep them in position. Smaller hooks are used for attaching linings to curtain tape.

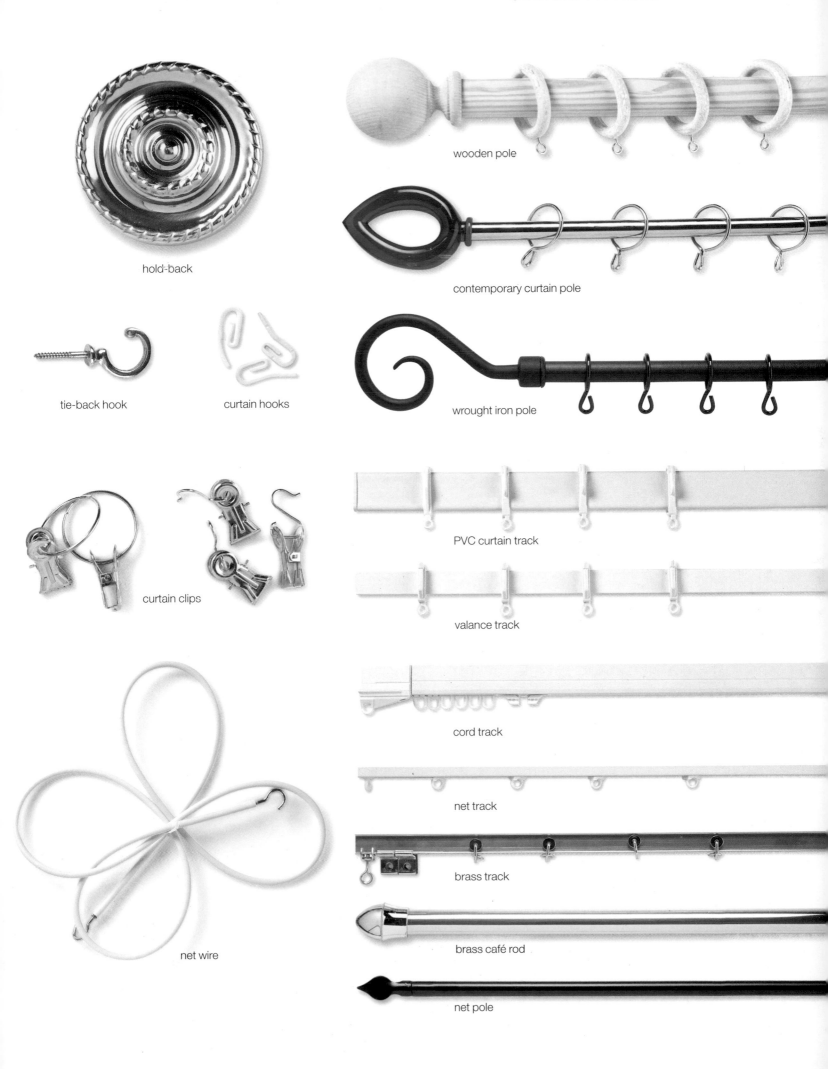

hold-back

wooden pole

contemporary curtain pole

tie-back hook

curtain hooks

wrought iron pole

curtain clips

PVC curtain track

valance track

cord track

net track

brass track

net wire

brass café rod

net pole

tailor-made curtains

Making curtains and blinds is an exciting and creative process that combines both artistic and practical skills. In addition to sewing, you will need to use some simple woodwork to complete some of the blinds and to make pelmet boards for hanging pelmets, valances, swags and tails. In general, this is simply a case of cutting a particular piece of wood to length. The wood used is all standard size and readily available in a DIY store or timber yard. Indeed, if you figure out the exact length required, the timber yard will cut it for you.

On the other hand, attaching the pelmet board to the wall is a job for the professionals. Every wall is different and there are special fittings designed for particular types of wall. In some cases there is only a certain area that can be drilled into because of a metal lintel or soft plaster and this will affect your measurements. Whatever fitting you choose, it will need to be strong enough to take the weight of the curtains and the pelmet board. It is important to get this right as an inadequate choice could damage the wall considerably.

left These curtains are not designed to be drawn, but to frame the view through the window and to allow light to fall on to the desk.

DECIDING ON A STYLE

Proportion is one of the most important aspects of curtain and blind making. The finished window treatment should blend in with all the other furnishings in a room and be of similar style. Dramatic swags and tails are ideal in a main reception area if there is sufficient height, but would be overpowering fitted over smaller kitchen or bathroom windows. Simple curtains and blinds in pretty colours soften the harsh lines and clinical appearance of these rooms and make them look more inviting.

The shape and position of the window need not limit your furnishing options as there are many ways to alter the window's appearance. Windows that are too wide or narrow can be disguised by keeping the curtains partly drawn on a short track, or fitted on track that extends more than 15 per cent on each side respectively. Curtains that need to have as much height as possible can be fitted to a pelmet board that is attached to the ceiling for maximum length.

LIGHT AND VIEW

Whatever style of window treatment you would like, take into consideration the view from the window and the amount of light that you want to come through. If the view is unattractive or the window looks out on to the street, sheer curtains or a flat blind can be hung inside the recess to provide screening or privacy. A dramatic view through a large window, on the other hand, will influence the colour choice of any fabric in the same way as a frame or mount can change the appearance of a picture.

Once you have chosen a particular style of curtain or blind, decide how and at what height it is going to be hung and if possible arrange to fit the curtain rail, pole or pelmet board before you begin to measure.

Further instructions for measuring and fitting blinds in particular are included at the end of this section.

MEASURING THE WINDOW

Measuring is the most important part of curtain-making. The best advice is to use a steel or wooden ruler and to double-check every measurement before

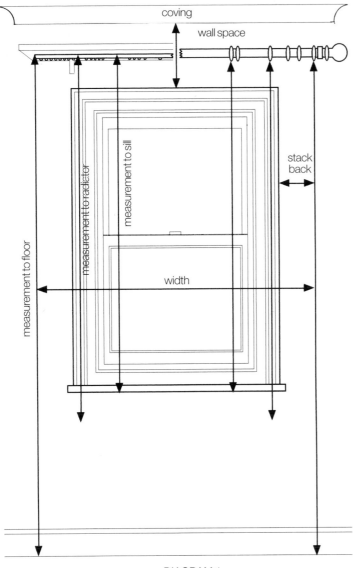

DIAGRAM 1

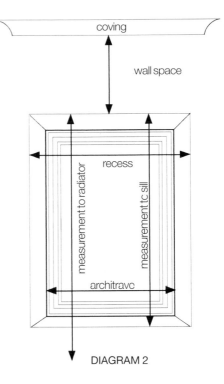

DIAGRAM 2

cutting out the fabric. Measurements are also required for working out the length of hardware (such as a curtain pole) and estimating the amount of fabric and trimmings you will need.

It is better to take every possible measurement at one time, rather than just those you think you will need. If your plans change, there will then be no need to re-measure. Measure each window individually, even if they appear to be the same size. If there is more than one window on a wall, measure the space between them so that you can plan for a picture or other decoration.

MEASURING EXISTING FITTINGS

If you are using existing tracks and fittings, the measuring is fairly straightforward but it is still essential to keep a record.

Curtain track or pole
- Measure the length of the track or pole and the distance away from the wall (the return).
- Measure the curtain length from the bottom of the curtain hooks to the windowsill, top of the radiator or the floor.

Pelmet board
In addition to the above, measure the length of the pelmet board and the return (from the front edge of the pelmet board to the wall). Consider whether you would like a decorative finish, such as box pleats at the corners, as this will affect the required fabric quantity.

Measuring bare windows
When measuring windows for the first time, take measurements in the middle and at each side in case the floor or ceiling is uneven.
- Measure from the ceiling or from the bottom of the coving to the floor.
- Measure the wall space from the ceiling or from the bottom of the coving to the top of the window or recess.
- Measure the length and width of the window, including the frame or the inside of the recess.
- Measure from the windowsill to the floor.
- Measure the space available on each side of the window for an extended curtain track. The curtain pole or track is usually 30 per cent longer than the width of the window.

curtain choices

With a curtain style in mind, the next stage is purely practical – how much fabric will be required?

DECIDING ON THE CURTAIN LENGTH

Curtains look very elegant if they are full-length, touching the floor or even draping on to the carpet. However, curtains that drape on to the floor have their disadvantages. They need to be re-arranged every time they are opened or closed, and they make vacuuming difficult. Pets love to use the comfortable "pools" of fabric as a bed!

below *Tab curtains should be hung above a door frame so that no light is visible between the tabs.*

Suitable lengths for short curtains are windowsill-length if they fit inside the recess, or radiator-length when they hang 10–15cm/4–6in below the sill. If the curtain is to be held back with tie-backs, add an extra 2.5–5cm/1–2in allowance.

THE CURTAIN TRACK OR POLE

Tracks for sheer and lightweight curtain fabrics can be fitted to the ceiling, or to the window frame inside a recess for a windowsill-length curtain. The track is therefore the width of the recess less 2–3cm/¾–1¼in to allow for fitting the hooks and curtains.

Curtain poles and tracks that are fitted outside the window recess are 30 per cent wider than the window.

This allowance, known as the "stack-back", enables the curtains to be pulled back to the edge of the window, allowing the maximum of light in during the day. Full or very bulky interlined curtains need slightly more stack-back, as do corded tracks and poles.

Solid metal lintels above a window can sometimes determine the position of the curtain pole. In general, the pole should be high enough to allow the top of the curtains to cover the top edge of the window. You need to decide on the style of the curtain at this stage as the curtains will hang at different heights if they have ties or tabs, or hang from curtain rings.

FITTING A PELMET BOARD

A bare curtain track is not very attractive and should, if possible, be fitted with a separate valance track, or secured to a pelmet board. The pelmet board is fitted to the wall space above the window and hangs down to cover the track. The height of the board depends on the proportions of the window – a pelmet or valance is usually one-fifth to one-sixth the length of the finished curtain. The pelmet board can be moved within the wall area above the window, but should ideally be fitted directly underneath the cornice or coving.

MAKING A PELMET BOARD

A pelmet board is simply a wooden plank 2cm/¾in thick and 15cm/6in wide. It should be the length of the curtain track, plus an average 10cm/4in curtain housing allowance on either side. If the curtains are extremely full, this allowance can increase to as much as 30cm/12in.

Brackets (which must be strong enough to hold the weight of the curtains and valance) are fitted flush with the back edge of the pelmet board. The curtain track is fitted 8cm/3in from the front edge. To allow the curtains to turn at right angles at the end to touch the wall, insert a large screw-eye to each back corner of the pelmet board and insert the last hook of the curtains at each end.

The front edge and sides of the pelmet board are covered in hook Velcro. Even if this is the self-adhesive kind, it should also be stapled to make it secure.

WORKING OUT FABRIC QUANTITIES

Once the pelmet board, curtain track or pole is in place, you can work (figure) out the amount of fabric required.

Calculating the drop

Use a wooden or steel ruler to measure the drop. Begin from the floor, radiator or windowsill, and measure up to the bottom of the hook on the curtain track or pole. This is the finished length of the curtain, to which you will have to add the hem and turn-down allowances. Both of these two measurements vary depending on the style of curtain and heading used, and you should refer to the individual instructions for each project. As a general guide, for the majority of curtains using a heading tape, add 15cm/6in hem allowance and 10cm/4in for the turn-down at the top.

Calculating the width

The length of the curtain pole and the fullness of the curtain determine the curtain width. Add extra allowances for an overlap arm and the return if you are using a pelmet board.
- For curtains on a pelmet board, add 10cm/4in for the return and overlap arm to each curtain.
- For a valance fitted to a pelmet board, measure along the front edge and down both sides.

above *Make sure the wall will support the weight of heavy curtain fabric as well as the pelmet board and always use suitable materials.*

CURTAIN WIDTHS

Different heading types use varying amounts of fabric, but these can be estimated fairly accurately. Work (figure) out the finished curtain width using the chart below, then add 10cm/4in side hem allowance.

Types of heading	Required width
Tie top or flat with clips	1½–2 times the width
Tab top	1–1½ times the width
Pencil pleats	2–2½ times the width
Pinch pleats or goblet tape	2 times the width
Box pleats	3 times the width
Hand-sewn headings	2–2½ times the width

getting started

Curtain fabric is normally 137cm/54in wide, and curtains are made with several lengths joined together. Divide the width of the fabric into the curtain width plus allowances to find the number of drops required. Multiply this number by two if there are two curtains. It is always better to round measurements up rather than down, and any length or drop should not be under half a width. If there are half-widths, join one half to the outside of each curtain.

Working with patterned fabric

The usable fabric width for curtain making may be slightly narrower if a design, check or stripe has to be matched. Match the fabric and measure the usable width before calculating the number of drops.

Buying the fabric

Once you have calculated the amount of fabric required, remembering to add the hem and turn-down allowances to each drop, take the measurements to the fabric shop. Choose your fabric and ask the sales assistant to double-check your measurements. Extra allowance will have to be made for a patterned fabric, but the sales assistant will be able to calculate the extra fabric required to match a design. As a general guide, add one design repeat for each drop. This additional fabric can add considerably to the cost of the curtains, particularly if the fabric has a large pattern repeat.

Before you begin

Check against your original sample that you have the right fabric and unroll it completely on a flat surface, to look for any flaws. Check the front and back of the fabric carefully.

Curtains hang better if the fabric is cut on the straight grain. On coarsely woven fabrics you can cut straight along a thread and some plain fabrics can be torn across, but there is always a risk that this will damage the fabric.

Snip into the selvage and pull one of the threads carefully so that the fabric gathers. Ease the gathers as far as you can and cut along the line. Work all the way across the fabric.

Fold the fabric in half and check that the corners meet. If not, match the corners and side seams and pin. Steam-press the fabric to straighten.

If the fabric is very off-grain, pull the adjacent sides apart either side of the corner, then press as before.

CUTTING THE FABRIC

Check the cutting length of each drop one last time, then measure up the selvage. Line the selvage up along the edge of the cutting table, and use a set square and metre (yard) stick to make a line at right angles across the fabric. A rotary cutter and quilter's ruler is a worthwhile investment for this as the fabric can be cut without marking a line.

Cutting patterned fabrics

Always cut complete pattern repeats so that they will lie across the hemline of the curtain. A part-repeat will be less noticeable hidden in the gathers or folds of a heading.

Remember to add the hem allowance below the pattern repeat before cutting out the fabric.

above *Fold the first length lengthways along the side seamline and lie it along the fabric, moving it until the design matches. Mark the length at both ends and cut as before.*

curtain construction

With the fabric in hand and your measurements carefully checked, you are ready to begin.

MAKING THE CURTAINS

Curtains are always made from the hem up. The side seams and hem are completed and any lining inserted, before the heading is attached. Complete the curtains according to the individual project instructions. The following is a rough guide to the order of stitching but should be read in conjunction with the project instructions.

Stitch the widths of fabric together with plain seams. Press the seams open. If the fabric has a design, slip-tack (baste) the seams before sewing. Fold under and then accurately measure and press the side seam and hem allowances.

Trim the lining to exactly the same width as the curtain at this stage. Fold up and press a double 5cm/2in hem along the bottom. Stitch the hem. Press under 2.5cm/1in down each side seam. With right sides together, pin the lining and curtain raw edges together. Stitch along the pressed line or slip-stitch along the fold.

Adding weights

Curtain weights are used to add extra weight to the hem of curtains, or in the corners of swags and tails.

They prevent a curtain from blowing about if the window or a door is open, and help the fabric to drape well.

1 Stitch the lead weight just above the fold in the corner of the hem. Take care not to stitch through to the front of the curtain.

2 Lengths of lead chain can be stitched along the fold of the hem. Oversew the hem, catching only a thread on the hemline.

Cutting the curtain to length

Once the curtain is complete, except for the top edge, it can be trimmed to the required length, ready for the heading. Work on a long table or on the floor.

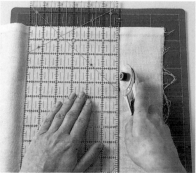

1 Fold the curtain in four, matching the corners, hem and side seams exactly.

2 Measure the length of the curtain drop, add the turn-over allowance for the particular heading you are using and mark the length with a pin.

3 Ideally use a quilter's ruler and rotary cutter to trim the curtain to length. Alternatively, mark a line at right angles with a set square and ruler.

Completing the heading

Curtains with heading tapes have long cords that are pulled up to gather the heading. These cords can be quite bulky and need to be stored neatly on the back of the curtain at the outside edge. Use either of these methods.

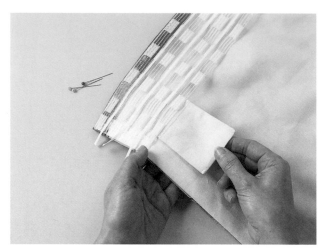

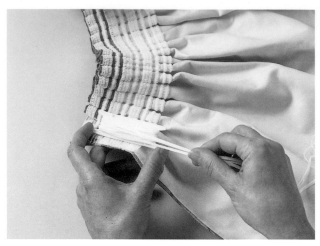

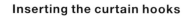

1 Cut an 8 x 15cm/3 x 6in piece of lining and stitch a narrow hem at one short end. Fold the lining in half widthways, right sides together, so that there is a 2cm/¾ in seam allowance above the hem. Stitch the side seams and turn through. Tuck the seam allowance under the tape and stitch in place.

2 Alternatively, you can buy a cord tidy to wrap the cords around. Hold the tidy against the heading tape and wrap the ends neatly around it.

Inserting the curtain hooks

Gather the heading tape up fully – it can be let out slightly later to fit the window. Insert a curtain hook in every fourth pleat along a pencil-pleated tape. Fancy heading tapes and hand-stitched headings have their own style of hook. Ask for the correct hooks at your furnishing fabric department.

above *Curtains with a contrast lining always look striking. Choose a colour that appears in the main fabric for best effect.*

left *Combining plain and pattern fabrics is a good way of making costly fabric that you like go further.*

MAKING A PATTERN FOR A VALANCE

Draw a paper template of the shape required. Pin the template over the top of the window to check how it looks. The centre depth should be approximately one-sixth of the finished length of the curtains, and the outside edges about 30–45cm/12–18in longer. Adjust the shape until you are satisfied.

Measure the length of the pelmet board and add twice the return (the side edge). Join the widths of fabric and lining together to make panels three times this width plus 3cm/1¼in seam allowance. Cut the panels to the required width.

Multiply the length of the return by three and add 1.5cm/⅝in hem allowance. Fold the lining panel in half and mark this point with pins in from the raw edges. Measure down from the top edge and mark the longest valance measurement.

Measure the midway depth on the original template, one quarter of the way across. Mark this length on the lining halfway between the other measurements. Join the marks in a gentle, smooth curve, keeping the line perpendicular to the fold and selvage at each end. Ensure the design is symmetrical and there are no awkward lines. When you are satisfied with the shape cut along the line.

above *Valances look attractive at tall windows, but use a lot of additional fabric.*

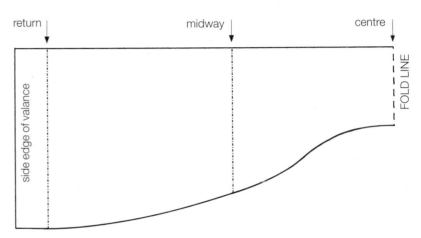

MAKING A PATTERN FOR A DRAPED SWAG

The centre of the swag should hang down to one-fifth of the length of the curtains. This is also the measurement for the short side of each tail. The long side of the tails should hang down one-third of the curtain length. Cut a wooden batten or put pins into your work surface to mark the length of the pelmet board. Pin a curtain weight chain to one mark and drape it around to the other mark so that the chain hangs down to one-fifth

of the length of the curtains in the middle. Measure the length of the chain between the marks.

Cut out the lining fabric twice the depth of the finished swag (i.e. two-fifths of the curtain length). The width should be twice the long side of the tail (i.e. two-thirds the curtain length) plus the length of the pelmet board. Transfer the measurements to the lining fabric as shown in the diagram. Join the outside marks with a straight line and the inside marks with a dotted line.

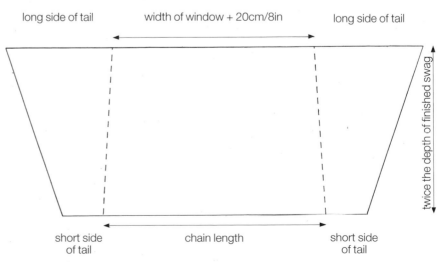

left *Draped swags use less fabric than valances and frame tall windows well.*

hanging curtains

Once you have completed the curtains, hang them as soon as possible to prevent them being creased. Never hang curtains alone as it is all too easy to lose your balance and fall from a step ladder. If there is a delay, place the completed curtains on the bed or over the banister, using a sheet to keep off the dust.

Count the number of hooks across the curtain and check there are a corresponding number of runners on the rail. Allow a hook for each screw-eye on a pelmet board. Find a step ladder that is tall enough for you to reach the top of the window easily.

below *These neatly dressed curtains are swept back in low tie-backs for a dramatic effect.*

Drape the curtain over your shoulder, with the heading tape in front. Hook the curtain to the rail, beginning at the outside edge. Don't begin in the centre as the entire weight of the curtain may cause the rail to buckle.

Hang a second curtain in the same way. Close the curtains and adjust the gathers on the tape until they are exactly the right length. Tie the cords together in a bow and secure them in a pocket or cord tidy.

DRESSING THE CURTAINS

All curtains hang much better if they are "dressed", or arranged, before use. This encourages them to fall in neat folds and helps the lining, interlining and main fabric to work as one fabric.

Open the curtains fully and begin in the middle of the right-hand leading edge. Tuck the outstretched fingers of your left hand behind the curtain and fold the curtain back over your fingers with your right hand to form a soft pleat. Keep working across the curtain, making finger-length folds of about 12cm/5in. Hold the pleats in place against your body. The outside edge of the curtain should end up facing the wall; if it doesn't, re-pleat, making the pleats slightly smaller or larger. Tie the pleated curtain loosely with a piece of seam tape. Repeat the process at the top and bottom of the curtain. If possible, leave the curtains for two or three days to "set" the pleats.

Fitting a tie-back hook

Be careful when fitting tie-back hooks to preserve the proportions of the curtains. On full-length curtains the hook is usually fitted about 95–100cm/37–39in from the floor. Ask a friend to hold the tie-back in position, blousing the fabric over the top. Stand back and decide if it looks right, adjusting it up or down until you are satisfied with the result.

right *Screw the tie-back hook into the wall, level with the outer edge of the curtain. Both ends of the tie-back can be fitted to the same hook, or a second hook can be attached 5cm/2in further in.*

making blinds

There are many different blinds you can choose, in all shapes and sizes to suit a wide variety of rooms and decorative styles. Some blinds such as roller blinds and Roman blinds are plain and are positioned flat to a window, whereas Austrian and London blinds are fuller and may have gathered headings.

MEASURING FOR A BLIND

Blinds can be fitted inside the recess of a window or on the outside. The instructions given earlier for measuring a window for curtains apply to blinds as well.

Inside the recess

If the blind will hang inside the recess, subtract 3cm/ 1¼in from the width to allow for the blind mechanism or cord. You do not need to allow for side hems on a roller blind, but check the individual project instructions for all other styles before cutting the fabric.

On the length, allow extra fabric for fitting a roller blind to the roller. Allow a hem allowance on other kinds of blind.

Outside the recess

Blinds that fit outside the recess should overlap on to the wall by at least 5cm/2in on either side. The blind can end at the windowsill, or can drop 10–15cm/4–6in below. This extra length can be particularly effective on an Austrian blind, cut slightly long so that the hem will still fall in scallops. The blind can be fitted at ceiling height or just above the window.

FITTING A BLIND

Blinds can be fitted to a blind track or to a specially prepared wooden batten. Most blinds can be fitted to a batten, but it is easier to use a ready-made track for Austrian or festoon blinds. The batten method is ideal for all other blinds and is simple to make without any specialist woodworking skills. The size of the battening will depend on the space available at the top of the window. Use 5 x 2.5cm/2 x 1in if possible, otherwise 2.5 x 2.5cm/1 x 1in, and cut the wood to the exact width of the finished blind. The wood can be painted to match the window frame or covered in the blind fabric, with the raw edges hidden on the back edge. Fold the fabric over the wood and staple it in position.

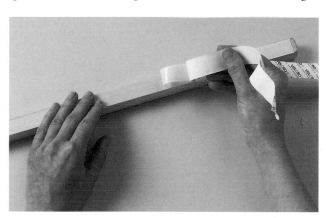

1 Velcro is indispensable for fitting blinds. It is a secure method for fitting and allows the blind to be removed for cleaning. Stick a strip of Velcro along the front edge of the batten and secure it with staples.

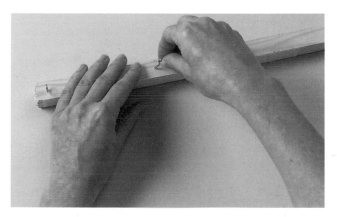

2 Lay the batten along the top edge of the blind and mark the position of the cords. Insert a large screw-eye at each mark along the bottom of the batten. Fit a screw-eye at the end of the batten where the cord will hang. Screw the batten to the top edge of the window frame inside the recess, or fit it with brackets in the wall space above the window. The blind can hang from just below the coving, at ceiling height or about 10cm/4in above the window.

Fitting a cleat

The cleat for securing the blind cord is usually fitted on the right-hand side of the window. It can be quite high up the wall, where it will be hidden in the fullness of a London or Austrian blind, or at windowsill height for a flat blind such as a Roman or roller blind.

choosing a heading tape

Heading tapes for curtains are now available in a wide range of styles to suit every possible situation. There are different widths for short and long curtains, and different tapes for attaching with curtains hooks or Velcro. Standard curtain tapes can be used with either curtain tracks or poles, and can be fixed or drawn. The more decorative styles of tape have special hooks to allow the curtains to hang as elegantly as possible.

Check when you buy the tape that you purchase the correct hooks. Velcro tapes are used for fixed curtains or valances. The Velcro can be attached to the edge of a pelmet board, on to a baton or even directly on a painted wall. With these tapes, the width of the curtain has to be pulled up to exactly the same width as the Velcro. Velcro tapes are ideal for unusual-shaped windows where it isn't possible to fit a curtain track.

Standard tape

This is the original heading tape. It is 2.5cm/1in wide and is usually attached 2.5–5cm/1–2in below the top of the curtain to create a soft frill that partly covers the pole or track. The curtain needs to be 1½–2 times the length of the track for a softly gathered heading. To attach, fold the tape over at the first pocket. Standard heading tape can be hung with standard curtain hooks.

Pencil pleats

The standard 8cm/3in pencil pleat tape is without doubt the most popular heading tape used today. Its neat pencil-width pleats are held firmly upright because of a special plastic weft thread woven into the tape. Use standard hooks in one of two rows of pockets for fitting to a curtain track or pole. The tape is also available as a Velcro tape for valances and fixed curtains.

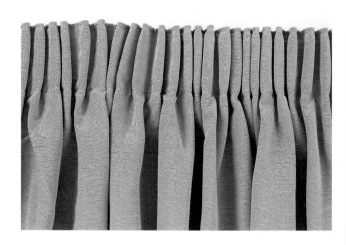

Deep pencil pleats

Full-length curtains without a valance look much more elegant with a deeper heading tape because the longer pencil pleats are in better proportion to the length of the curtains. Both the 8cm/3in tape and this 14cm/5½in tape require 2–2½ times the length of the track for optimum fullness, allowing the pleats to lie neatly side by side. The deeper tape has three rows of pockets.

Triple pleat

Triple pleat tape creates one of the most elegant curtain headings and looks equally good whether the curtain is open or closed. There are several widths of triple pleat tape for all lengths of curtain. When attaching the tape, cut the tape in the centre of a group of pleats and pull the cords out to where they emerge. Triple-pleated curtains require special hooks for hanging.

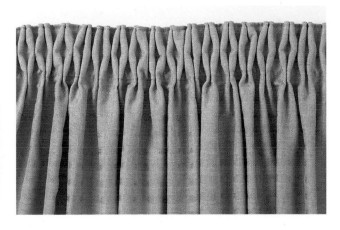

Box pleat

This heading tape is one of the most formal and is used primarily for valances as it is not recommended for curtains that can be drawn. Box pleating tape comes in a standard 8cm/3in width and requires three times the length of the track. Cut the tape in the centre of a group of pleats and pull the cords out to where they emerge from the tape. Special hooks are used for hanging.

Trellis tape

Trellis tape is an attractive variation of the standard pencil pleat. It has half-length pleats that lock together just like clasped fingers. It is available in both 2.5cm/1in and 8cm/3in widths and each requires 1½–2 times the track length. Trellis tape uses standard curtain hooks for hanging. The wider tape has two rows of pockets to allow the curtain track or pole to be partly hidden if required.

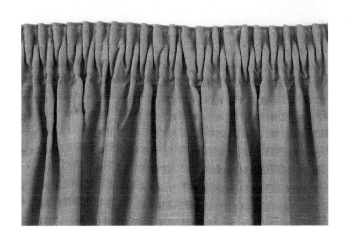

Smocking

This decorative heading tape creates a soft, smocked effect across the top of the curtain. It uses standard curtain hooks and track, and has two rows of pockets for using with a curtain pole or track. Smocked headings require 2½ times the length of the track but are only suitable for valances or fixed curtains. The tape should not be pulled up too tightly or the smocked effect will be lost.

basic curtain

The simplest and quickest way to make a curtain is to create a flat rectangle, with machine-stitched hems. The finished curtain can be decorated with simple embroidery patterns such as the running stitch spirals shown here (see basic techniques). It is designed to be hung with curtain clips.

calculating the fabric

Flat curtains only need 1½ times the width for fullness. Remember to divide the finished width by half if there are two curtains. Add 8cm/3in to the width and 26cm/10in to the length for hems.

you will need

- fabric
- sewing kit

tips for basic curtain

- Space the clips every 10–15cm/4–6in.
- After making the curtains, mark any embroidery design with a vanishing marker and stitch with a tapestry needle and crochet cotton or coton à broder.

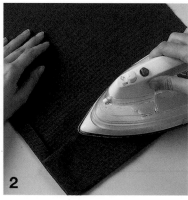

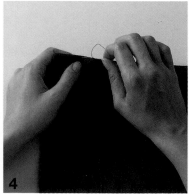

1 Turn under and press a 2cm/¾in hem down each side of the curtain fabric. Fold the hem under again to make a double hem and press.

2 Check the curtains for length, and turn under and press a double 8cm/3in hem along the bottom edge.

3 Stitch the side seams, stitching close to the inside fold. Textured fabrics such as velvet or satin can be slip-hemmed by hand.

4 Stitch the bottom hem then slip-stitch the sides by hand. Mark the length of the curtain and stitch a 5cm/2in double hem along the top edge.

tie-top curtain

An alternative way to hang a flat curtain is with decorative ties along the top edge. Make up the curtain in the same way as the basic curtain, but mark the required length up from the bottom hem and cut 1.5cm/⅝in above this mark. The ties can be attached into a lining or using a facing. The length of the ties depends on how far the top of the curtain will hang below the curtain rail and whether they are tied in a knot or a bow.

calculating the fabric

Tie-top curtains require 1½–2 times the window width for fullness. Add hem allowances as for the basic curtain. Check the length of the tie, usually about 60cm/24in and add this to the length of fabric required. The ties are cut vertically across the fabric so that the pattern matches.

you will need

- **fabric**
- **sewing kit**

tip for tie-top curtain
If the centre of each tie is offset when attached to the curtain, the bow will lie at the top of the curtain pole.

1 To make the ties, cut 5cm/2in-wide strips of fabric, double the required length of the ties plus 2cm/¾in seam allowance. Press under 1cm/½in along each edge. Fold the ties in half lengthways and stitch close to the edge.

2 Make sufficient ties for one to be spaced every 15–20cm/6–8in along the top of the curtain. Fold each tie in half and pin in position on the right side of the curtain, along the top edge.

3 For the facing, cut an 8cm/3in-wide strip of fabric to fit across the width of the curtain plus 3cm/1¼in seam allowance. Pin it right side down over the ties and stitch along the top edge. Fold the facing over to the inside of the curtain.

4 Press 1.5cm/⅝in along the sides of the facing to the wrong side. Slip-stitch the sides of the facing, and hem or stitch the bottom edge.

tab-top curtain

A deep border and facing make it much easier to attach tabs, which are particularly suitable for heavier-weight curtains. The depth of the border depends on personal taste but should be in proportion to the length of the curtain. Stitch the hem and side seams of the main body of the curtain before adding the border and add a lining at this stage, if required.

calculating the fabric

Plan the depth of the border and the length of the curtain. Allow 10cm/4in on the width and 16.5cm/6½in lengthwise for the hem and seam allowances. Cut two contrast border panels, adding 1.5cm/⅝in seam allowance all round. The average tab is 40cm/16in long. Allow an extra ½m/½yd to cut the tabs.

you will need

- fabric A
- fabric B
- sewing kit

tip for tab-top curtain

Space the tabs approximately every 15–20cm/6–8in.

1 Using contrast fabric, cut tabs twice the required finished width and length plus 3cm/1¼in seam allowance. Fold each tab in half lengthways, right sides together, and stitch along the long edge . Trim the seams and press open. Turn the tabs right side out and press, with the seam down the centre back.

2 Using contrast fabric, cut a border panel the required depth and the same width as each curtain, adding 3cm/1¼in seam allowance to both measurements. With right sides together, stitch the panel to the top of each curtain piece. Open out and press. With the seams to the inside, space the folded tabs along the top of the border on the right side. Align the raw edges.

3 For the facing, cut a second panel the same size as the border from contrast fabric. With right sides together and raw edges aligned, pin in position on top of the border, and stitch along the top edge. Press the seam flat. Turn the facing over to the wrong side of the curtain. Turn the side edges in to match the width of the curtain. Press.

4 Turn under the lower edge of the facing in line with the stitching and pin. Slip-stitch the side edges of the border and hem the facing to the stitches.

1

2

3

4

mitred corner curtain

Fabrics that are equally attractive on both sides are ideal for making this flat curtain. The wrong side will show on the mitred hems and where the curtain is folded over to create a mock valance. The finished curtain is hung from clips.

calculating the fabric

The depth of the mock valance is entirely personal, but a good guide is ⅙–⅛ the finished length. Allow 1½ times the track length for fullness. Add the valance depth to the finished length of the curtains and allow 15cm/6in on each edge for the hems.

you will need

- **reversible fabric**
- **sewing kit**

tip for mitred corner curtain

The length of the curtain can be adjusted by changing the depth of the valance.

1 If you are using a patterned fabric, the width of the hem all round the curtain will depend on the depth of the pattern. Fold the fabric along a line in the pattern and mark the hem width, approximately 8cm/3in depending on the pattern repeat. Trim 1.5cm/⅝in away from this mark.

2 Decide which side of the fabric you wish to be the right side and place it facing outwards. Turn over a double hem on each side and the top and bottom edge and press.

3 Open out the hems and fold diagonally across the corner at the first crease marks. Trim 1cm/½in in from the fold to reduce bulk.

4 Refold the double hems and press. Pin and tack (baste) the hems then stitch close to the inside fold. Slip-stitch the mitred corners.

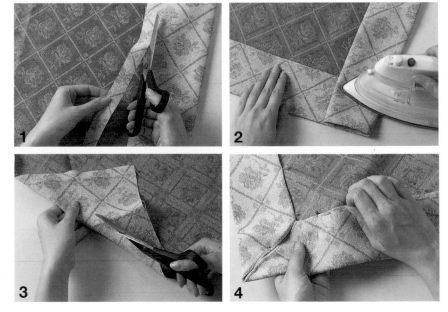

lined flat curtain

A fitted lining will improve the look of a basic curtain, making it hang better and will protect the body of the fabric from fading. Linings help prolong the life of the curtain and when worn can be replaced more economically than replacing an entire set of curtains.

calculating the fabric

Allow 1½–2 times the finished track length depending on the amount of fullness required. Add 10cm/4in to the width and 20cm/8in to the length for hems. The lining is the same width as the finished curtain and 13cm/5in longer.

you will need

- **fabric**
- **lining**
- **sewing kit**

tip for lined flat curtain

Insert a weight into the bottom corners of each curtain.

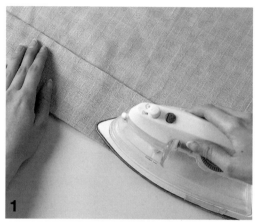

above *Attach clips every 10–15cm/4–6in.*

1 Press under a single 5cm/2in hem on the side seams of the curtain fabric, then press under a double 8cm/3in hem on the bottom edge. Insert a pin on the side hem at the top of the bottom hem.

2 Open out the hems and fold the fabric diagonally, with the marker pin at the top of the new fold, and the bottom of the side fold meeting the lower new fold. Press and refold, then blind-hem the bottom (see basic techniques).

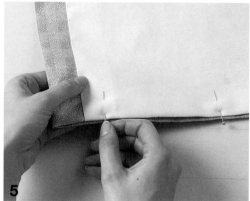

3 Cut out the lining the same width as the finished curtain and 13cm/5in longer. Press under a 5cm/2in double hem along the bottom and stitch.

4 Open out the side hem. With right sides together, pin one side of the lining down one side hem of the curtain so that the top of the lining hem is level with the curtain hem.

5 Repeat with the other side of the curtain and lining, and stitch 2.5cm/1in from the raw edge of the lining on both sides. Press the seams towards the lining. Turn the curtain through to the right side. Turn under 5cm/2in along the top edge of the lining and press so that the raw edges are between the layers. Pin the lining just below the curtain fabric and slip-hem in place.

lined tab-top curtain

This method of adding tabs is ideal if you do not want stitching showing on the right side.
It is particularly suitable for fabrics such as velvet or satin.

calculating the fabric

Allow 1½–2 times the finished track length depending on the amount of fullness required. Add 10cm/4in to the width and 20cm/8in to the length for hem and seam allowances. Cut the lining the same width as the finished curtain and 7cm/2¾in longer. Allow 0.5m/½yd fabric for the tabs.

you will need

- **fabric**
- **lining**
- **sewing kit**

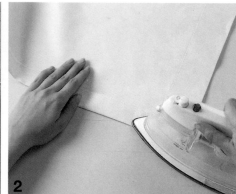

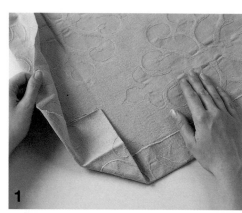

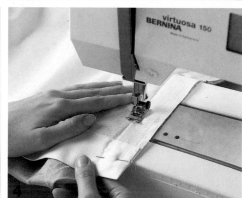

1 Press under a single 5cm/2in hem on the side seams of the curtain fabric, then press under a double 8cm/3in hem on the bottom edge. Fold and press the mitred corner. Blind-hem the bottom hem (see basic techniques).

2 Cut out the lining the same width as the finished curtain and 13cm/5in longer. Press under a 5cm/2in double hem along the bottom and stitch. Turn under 2.5cm/1in down the sides.

3 Pin the lining to the side seams with raw edges together, and so that the top of the hems are in line.

4 Turn the curtain through and stitch the side seams along the pressed fold line.

5 Make the required number of tabs (see tab-top curtain). Pin the first tab level with the pressed fold at the side of the curtain. Space the other tabs equally across the top of the curtain. Stitch along 2cm/¾in from the top edge.

6 Turn the curtain through and press the top edge. Stitch 2.5cm/1in from the top of the curtain for extra strength, if desired. Slip-stitch the mitre and hem along the bottom edge of the lining for 2.5cm/1in to hold it in place.

café curtain

A café curtain forms an attractive screen across the bottom half of a window. To find the length, secure a curtain pole halfway up the window. Measure from the top of the curtain pole to the windowsill.

to make the pattern

Enlarge the template at the back of the book, adding as many tabs as necessary to achieve the required width. Fold the tabs over level with the bottom of the curved edges. Measure the finished length of the curtain from the top fold and cut off the excess paper.

you will need

- **paper and pencil to make a pattern**
- **fabric**
- **contrast lining fabric**
- **lightweight iron-on interfacing**
- **iron-on fusible bonding web**
- **self-cover button kit**
- **sewing kit**

tip for café curtain
Slip-stitch the hem if you do not have any fusible bonding web.

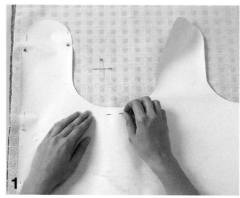

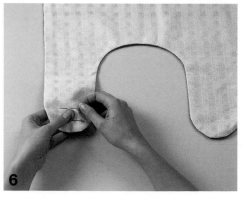

1 Measure the size of the template and add 5cm/2in to the width and length. Cut a piece of main and contrast lining fabric this size and another 18cm/7in strip the same width in contrast fabric. Pin the template to the two large pieces and cut out adding 1.5cm/⅝in seam allowances all round.

2 Cut 13.5cm/5¼in from the bottom of the main curtain panel. Press under a 1.5cm/⅝in seam along the top edge of the contrast border and pin then slip-tack to the main curtain fabric. Stitch and press the seam towards the border.

3 Cut a band of lightweight interfacing 30cm/12in wide and iron to the wrong side of the main fabric. Trim the excess around the curved edges.

4 Pin the lining and main fabric panels with right sides together, and stitch around the curved edges and down the side seams. Notch the outward facing curves and snip into the inward facing curves.

5 Turn through and ease out the curves carefully before pressing. Turn under 1.5cm/⅝in along the lower edge of the curtain and the lining and press the two hems together using iron-on fusible bonding web.

6 Cover the required number of buttons following the instructions on the packet. Mark the position of the buttonholes on the end of each tab. Stitch the buttonholes. Fold the tabs over level with the bottom of the curves and stitch a button in line with the buttonhole. Fold over the curtain pole and button the tabs.

curtain to hang from a rod or wires

A softly gathered curtain is often used as screening behind kitchen cupboards, glass-fronted wardrobes (closets) or French windows. The curtain is stretched between two wires or rods that are screwed into the reverse side of the door 5cm/2in above and below the panels.

calculating the fabric

The width of fabric required depends on the weight of the fabric and the effect you want to create. In general, allow twice the width for a lightweight fabric and 1½ times for medium curtain weight. The length of the fabric is the distance between the curtain rods or wires at the top and bottom plus 20cm/8in hem allowance.

you will need

- **fabric**
- **curtain rods or curtain wires**
- **sewing kit**

tip for curtain to hang from a rod or wires
If the fabric is the correct width, use the selvage rather than make a hem.

1 Measure between the curtain rods and cut the fabric to this length plus 20cm/8in for hems to encase the wire. At each side, press under and stitch 1cm/½in double hems. Press under a double 5cm/2in hem along the top and bottom edges.

2 Stitch the top and bottom hems close to the inside folded edge, reverse-stitching at each end to reinforce the stitching.

3 To make the casing for the wire, stitch 1cm/½in away from the first row of stitches. If you are using a curtain rod, adjust the size of the casing to fit.

separate lining

Curtains last much longer if they are lined as the lining protects the fabric from sunlight and damp. Many curtains have a fitted lining but you can make a separate lining to attach to curtains with a heading tape. Usually the lining is attached to the bottom row of pockets on the curtain heading tape with separate hooks.

above *Separate linings can be added to any type of curtain to help prolong the life of the fabric.*

calculating the fabric

A separate lining doesn't need to be as full as the body of the curtain. One-and-half times the width is sufficient. Cut the lining 5cm/2in longer than the finished curtain. If you need to join two or more lengths of lining fabric to fit a large window, stitch flat seams and press them open.

you will need
- **lining**
- **heading tape**
- **sewing kit**

1 Press under a 5cm/2in double hem along the bottom edge and a 1cm/½in double hem down both sides of the lining. Stitch in place and press.

2 Pull out 4cm/1½in of the cords at one end of the heading tape and knot the ends. Trim the cord ends.

3 Tuck the top edge of the lining between the two flaps along the lower edge of the tape and pin. Fold under the knotted ends of the tape and stitch across the tape to secure the cords.

4 Stitch along the lower edge of the tape from the right side. The underside of the tape is slightly longer so that it will be caught in the stitching. Gather the lining in as far as it will go, then loosen the gathers until it fits across the curtain. Insert curtain hooks through the loops and attach to the tape on the curtain.

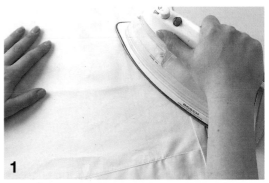

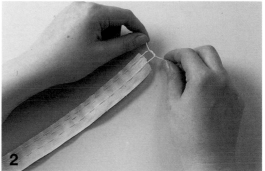

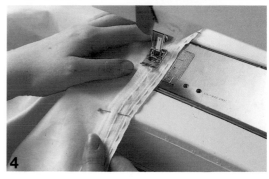

unlined curtain using heading tape

Heading or curtain tape is a popular way to hang curtains and is available in various styles to create different effects. Where you cut the tape depends on the type of tape. The pinch pleat tape shown here should be cut in the centre of a group of pleats at the edge of the curtain that will come to the centre of the window. The second curtain should have the loose cords of the tape at the other side. Be sure to purchase the correct curtain hooks for the tape you are using.

calculating the fabric

Measure the required curtain length and add 20cm/8in hem and heading allowance. Check the fullness ratio for your heading tape and add 8cm/3in for hems and 3cm/1¼in for any seam.

you will need

- fabric
- heading tape
- curtain weights
- cord tidy or cord pocket
- sewing kit

tip for unlined curtain using heading tape
Use pencil pleat or standard heading tape for an alternative look.

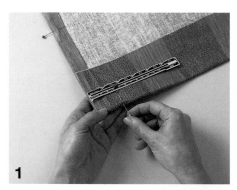

1 Press under a 2cm/¾in double hem down each side of the curtain fabric. Turn up and press a 8cm/3in double hem along the bottom edge. Insert a pin to mark the top of the bottom hem. Open out the hems and insert a pin 4cm/1½in in from the side edge.

2 Fold over the bottom hem diagonally between the pins and press flat.

3 Refold the side, then the bottom hems to make an uneven mitre corner, as shown, and press.

4 Slip-hem both side hems, catching only one or two threads of the main curtain fabric so that the stitching is almost invisible on the right side.

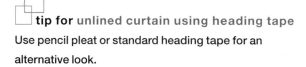

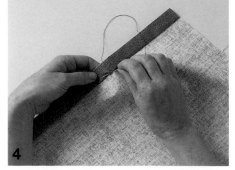

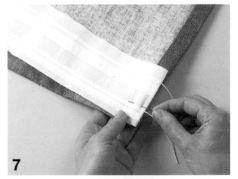

5 Fold the bottom hem back on itself so that 5mm/¼ in shows above the curtain fabric. Blind-hem, taking tiny stitches into the main curtain fabric and a longer stitch through the hem.

6 Tuck a weight into the hem at each bottom corner and stitch in place. Slip-stitch the mitred corners closed with invisible stitches.

7 Cut the curtain to the required length plus 1.5cm/⅝ in seam allowance at the top. Fold over the top seam allowance and press. Turn the curtain tape over at one side, leaving the cords free, and pin to the edge of the curtain. Make sure the tape is the right way up. Pin the tape 3mm/⅛ in from the top of the curtain. When you reach the other end of the curtain, trim the tape, allowing a little to turn under. Pull out the cords and tie together in a knot. Turn the end of the tape under and pin.

8 Stitch along the long sides of the tape, stitching both lines in the same direction. Stitch across both ends, but keep the cords free on the outside edge of each curtain.

to finish

Carefully pull up the pleats, using your thumb and fingers to support the tape. Hold the loose cords in one hand or tie them around a door handle. Keep working the pleats along the cords until the whole curtain is evenly pleated. Tie the cords in a slip knot, then tie the ends around a cord tidy or tuck them in a cord pocket. Insert a curtain hook into two adjacent loops at the back of each set of pleats.

attaching a permanent lining

Hand stitching a lining into a curtain gives a more professional finish. The lining is attached to the curtain with a series of parallel lines of lock stitch, which prevent the two layers from separating. Here standard curtain tape makes the curtain hang in soft, casual folds.

you will need
- fabric
- lining
- sewing kit

tips for attaching a permanent lining
- Contrasting colour linings work well and can be used on flamboyant curtains where the lining may show, for example, where the curtain is held part way down over a hold-back.
- Cut the lining to the same width as the finished curtain and 13cm/5in longer.

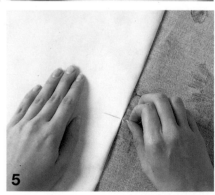
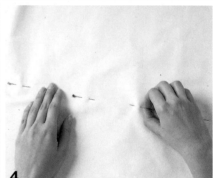

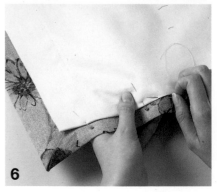

1 Press under a 5cm/2in single hem along both sides of the curtain. Turn up and press an 8cm/3in double hem along the bottom edge and mitre the corner (see basic techniques). Secure the edges of the side hems with herringbone stitch, catching just one or two threads on the main curtain so that the stitching is invisible on the right side.

2 Insert a weight into each corner and secure the bottom hem in place using blind hem stitch. On the wrong side, mark parallel lines with tailor's chalk down the curtain, midway across every width of fabric.

3 Cut out the lining to the same width as the curtains. Turn up and stitch a 5cm/2in double hem along the bottom edge. Turn in and press 2.5cm/1in down each side.

4 With wrong sides together, pin the lining to one folded edge of the curtain, then fold it back as far as the chalk line. Pin the lining and curtain fabric together along the chalk line, then tack (baste) along the line of pins, removing the pins as you go.

5 Work lock stitch down the fold to attach the lining to the curtain. Repeat the process for each chalk mark or seam until the lining is lock-stitched in place.

6 Slip-stitch each side of the lining to the curtain. Hem along the bottom for 2.5cm/1in so that the lining will not billow out if the window is open.

interlined curtain

Interlined curtains look substantial and luxurious, even if the curtains are made from lightweight fabric. Interlining or "bump" is a special cotton or mixed fibre wadding (batting) that is often added to door curtains, to insulate a room against draughts (drafts) and to absorb noise. It is available in a range of thicknesses, so hold the curtain fabric against the interlining to see how it affects the drape and appearance before deciding which to buy.

calculating the fabric

Interlined curtains do not need to be as full as ordinary curtains because of the bulk of the interlining. This heavyweight curtain is completed with a pencil pleat tape and requires only 1½ times the track length. Add 20cm/8in to the length for hems and turn-in allowance. Cut the borders twice the finished width, adding 20cm/8in to the length. Cut the interlining the same length, adding twice the border width to the width of the main curtain fabric.

you will need

- **fabric**
- **contrasting fabric**
- **interlining**
- **lining**
- **curtain weight**
- **sewing kit**

tip for interlined curtain

To join widths of interlining overlap the edges and secure with herringbone stitch.

1 Using contrast fabric, cut out a border panel twice the required finished width for each curtain. With right sides together and raw edges aligned, pin the border down the inside edge of the curtain fabric. Stitch in place with a 1.5cm/⅝in seam allowance. Press the seam open.

2 Cut out a piece of interlining to fit the size of the opened-out curtain fabric and place it on top. Turn under a 5cm/2in turning on the interlining down the border edge of the curtain. Lock-stitch along the fold to secure the interlining.

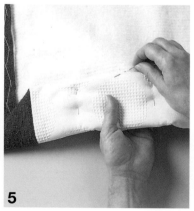
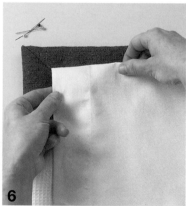

3 Fold the interlining back and lock-stitch the interlining in the centre of every width of fabric and down each seam. Cut off the interlining 8cm/3in from the bottom of the curtain and trim the corner, as shown, to reduce bulk.

4 Turn in the inside edge of the curtain and work a row of herringbone stitch into the interlining, close to the raw edge.

5 Turn up the bottom hem and pin, folding the corner into a neat mitre. Stitch a weight into the corner then hem the curtain fabric to the interlining.

6 Prepare the lining and pin the side seams. Mark, pin and lock-stitch every 30–50cm/12–20in across the lining (see attaching a permanent lining). Slip-hem the side seams. Hem along the bottom for 2.5cm/1in to secure. Trim the curtain to length and attach the curtain tape.

gathered valance with a shaped edge

A gathered valance is a soft, attractive way to finish curtains. It can be a short version of a curtain, or it can have a shaped lower edge. The valance can be decorated with binding, braid or another trimming to emphasize the curved shape of the bottom of the valance.

calculating the fabric

A valance is usually fuller than the curtain – normally three times the length of the track or pelmet board. Measure the length of the pelmet board and add twice the return (the distance to the wall) and multiply by three to calculate the width. The length of a straight valance is one-sixth of the curtain length. Make the pattern before calculating the fabric for a shaped valance. Buy 1m/1yd contrast fabric for the binding.

you will need

- **paper pattern**
- **fabric**
- **contrast or toning fabric**
- **8cm/3in heading tape**
- **lining**
- **sewing kit**

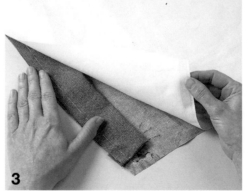

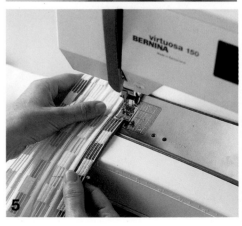

making the valance

You can make a valance with any style of Velcro curtain heading tape and make the lower edge straight or curved. To make a pattern for a shaped valance follow the instructions on page 19.

1 Join sufficient widths of fabric together to make a strip three times the width of the window. Adjust the depth of the pattern, taking the depth of the finished lower binding from the top edge. With right sides together fold the fabric in half. Draw around the pattern. Cut along the marked line.

2 Cut and join sufficient 13cm/5in-wide bias strips to fit along the curved edge of the valance. Press in the short ends. Fold the strip in half lengthways, wrong sides together and pin along the lower edge of the valance, raw edges aligned, beginning and ending 1.5cm/⅝in from both ends. Tack (baste) the binding to the valance.

3 Cut the lining using the valance pattern and place it on top of the binding, right sides together. Stitch the side seams and along the lower edge, leaving 1.5cm/⅝in seam allowance. Trim across the corners and turn through. Press the side seams and bottom edge.

4 Pin a 5cm/2in-wide strip of straight binding along the top edge of the valance and stitch, leaving 1.5cm/⅝in seam allowance. Press the binding away from the valance. Fold in the ends, then turn the binding over to the reverse side.

5 Stitch Velcro heading tape to the top edge of the valance on the wrong side. Knot the tape cords at one end, then pull up the tape as far as possible. Ease out the gathers to fit the window.

hand-pleated valance

Hand pleating is a simple way to create elegant triple or French pleats for the top of a valance or curtain. As there is no bulky heading tape, curtains with a hand-pleated heading will pull back into a smaller space. The effect is similar to a triple-pleat heading tape, but with this professional method there is no stitching on the right side and the pleats can be spaced to line up with stripes or patterns in the fabric. You can use any deep heading tape as an alternative.

calculating the fabric

For perfect proportions, a valance is usually one-sixth of the length of the finished curtains. The width required for a hand-pleated finish is 2–3 times the finished width, but will depend on the fabric pattern. Plan the pleats to make the best use of any stripes or pattern in the fabric. The pleats normally use 15cm/6in of fabric, with a 13cm/5in gap between them. Leave approximately 8cm/3in before the end pleats on a straight valance, and 23cm/9in if the valance is to be fitted to a pelmet board.

you will need

- fabric
- lining fabric
- 8cm/3in wide iron-on buckram
- self-cover button kit
- sewing kit

tip for hand-pleated valance

Make the curtains with a pencil tape heading so that they hang elegantly below the valance.

1 Cut the fabric 8cm/3in deeper than the finished valance, and the required width plus 1.5cm/⅝in seam allowance. Cut the lining the same width but 5cm/2in shorter. Stitch the lining to the bottom edge of the valance and press the seam open. Fold the fabrics wrong sides together so that all edges align and press the bottom edge.

2 With right sides together, stitch the side seams. Turn through, then press under 1.5cm/⅝in on the top edge of both the fabric and lining. Cut a piece of iron-on buckram to fit the length of the fabric and tuck it under the pressed turning, with the adhesive side facing the lining.

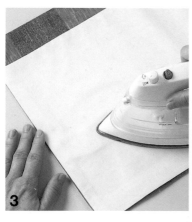

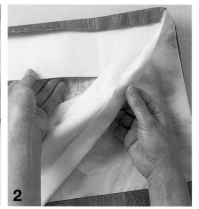

3 Smooth out the fabric and roll the seams so that they are directly on the edge. Press the lining to fuse it to the buckram.

4 Mark the return (the distance from the front of the pelmet board to the wall), the gaps and the pleat widths across the fabric. Fold the valance, matching the first two pleat marks, and stitch the pleat to the depth of the buckram only. Reverse stitch at each end.

5 Hold the centre of the fold and push down to form three equal pleats. Catch the top of the pleats in the centre with invisible hand stitches.

6 On the right side, oversew the pleats together at the bottom of the buckram. Cover buttons with matching or contrast fabric, using a button kit, and stitch on to the pleats to hide the oversewing stitches. On the wrong side, hand stitch loop Velcro along the top edge for hanging.

hard pelmet

A hard pelmet looks very impressive in a formal room. It can be any shape, but simple lines such as a soft curve or plain, straight edge are more modern. The most suitable backing board is 3mm/⅛in thick hardboard or plywood; you can use heavyweight buckram, but it is sensitive to atmospheric changes and may buckle if placed above a radiator. As a general rule, the depth of the pelmet is approximately one-sixth of the length of the curtains. Draw a paper template of the proposed shape and pin it over the top of the window to see how it will look. Adjust the shape until you are satisfied.

calculating the fabric

Decide on the finished depth of the contrast borders at the top and bottom. Measure the depth of the pelmet board and add 3cm/1¼in seam allowance, then subtract the depth of both borders. Cut out the main fabric to this measurement and add the length of the pelmet board plus twice the return, plus 30cm/12in. If the fabric needs to be joined, stitch half-widths at each side of one full width and press the seams flat.

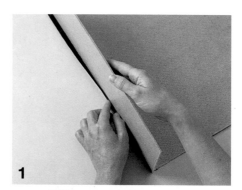

you will need

- pencil and paper
- 3mm/⅛in hardboard or plywood
- jigsaw
- carpet tape
- interlining
- multi-purpose adhesive
- contrast fabric
- fabric
- lining
- staple gun
- curved upholstery needle
- Velcro
- sewing kit

tip for making a **hard pelmet**
Interlining is not absolutely essential but gives a much better finish.

1 Using a jigsaw, cut a piece of hardboard or plywood the required shape for the main front piece of the pelmet. Cut two side panels the same depth as the outside edge and the length of the return, i.e. the distance the pelmet is away from the wall, (usually 15cm/6in). Attach the side panels to the board, using carpet tape down both inside edges.

2 Cut out a piece of interlining slightly larger than the pelmet board. Stick it to the front, using multi-purpose adhesive. Allow to dry, then trim the interlining flush with the sides.

3 Cut two strips of contrast fabric twice the depth of each finished border and 30cm/12in longer than the length of the board. With right sides together, pin and stitch the borders to the top and bottom of the main fabric, using 1.5cm/⅝in seam allowances.

4 Cut out the lining fabric the same size as the front of the board plus 1.5cm/⅝in seam allowance on all sides. Trim the lower border to the finished size plus 1.5cm/⅝in seam allowance. Pin the lining centrally along this edge and stitch.

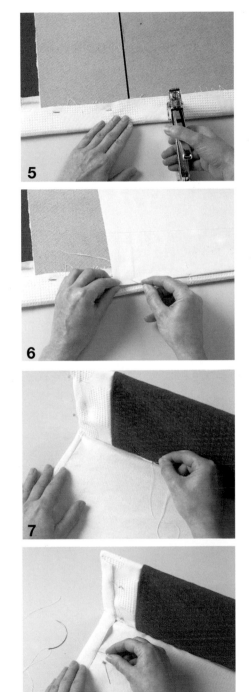

5 Place the pelmet fabric right side down on a flat surface. Place the board on top, with the bottom edge along the lining seam. Stretch the top border gently over the board and secure with 5mm/¼in staples into the back of the board.

6 Pull the lining over the back of the board, turn under the top edge and pin to the fabric at the top. From the right side, check that the borders are an equal size and straight. Hem or staple the lining along the top edge.

7 Fold over the fabric at the short end of the board and hold the end at right angles. Turn under the raw edges and pin. Using a curved upholstery needle, hand stitch the main fabric to the lining along the corner seam.

8 Pin a strip of loop Velcro along the top edge and hand stitch along both sides. Cut a 15cm/6in-wide pelmet board to fit inside the pelmet, at the top, then stick hook Velcro to the front and side edges. Secure with staples every 5–8cm/2–3in.

draped swag and tails

The simplest form of swag and tails is a trapezoid panel of fabric long enough to drape between hold-backs, with the tails hanging down each side. It looks most elegant when the top edge is fixed to a pelmet board and the tails fall over hold-backs on either side of tall narrow windows, such as French doors.

calculating the fabric

The two measurements required are the finished drop of the curtains and the length of the pelmet board, which usually extends 10cm/4in on each side of the window. Use these measurements to make a pattern for the swag following the instructions on page 19.

you will need

- **pattern**
- **fabric**
- **contrast fabric**
- **curtain weights and chain**
- **fabric tape**
- **pelmet board covered with calico**
- **staple gun**
- **sewing kit**

tip for draped swag and tails
Make matching hold-backs using either the main fabric or the contrast lining.

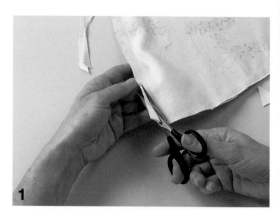

1 Using the pattern, cut out the swag shape in the main and contrast fabric adding 1.5cm/⅝in seam allowance all around. Make sure the fabric is the right way up, with the pelmet edge at the top, and centre any pattern before cutting. Place the two fabrics right sides together and stitch around the edge, with 1.5cm/⅝in seam allowance leaving a gap at the top edge for turning. Trim across the corners to reduce bulk.

2 Press the seams open, reaching as far as possible into the corners. Turn the swag through. Roll the seams until they are right on the edge and press. Drop a weight into the end of the tails and slip-stitch the gap closed.

3 Transfer the dotted line on the pattern to the wrong side of the swag. Insert pins along this line then tack (baste) to mark the line.

4 Pleat the swag along the tacked lines, beginning at the front edge and forming concertina (accordion) pleats about 10cm/4in deep across the fabric. Tie the pleats on the tacked line loosely with a piece of fabric tape. Pleat the other end in the same way.

5 Make the pelmet board following the guidelines in the introduction. Cover the pelmet board in calico or spare curtain fabric and fit in position. Attach the hold-backs to each side of the board.

6 Lift the swag into position so that the ties are behind the hold-backs. Staple the top edge of the swag to the top front edge of the pelmet board. Pull out the tapes and gently twist the swag behind the hold-backs until the tails are facing forward as shown.

formal fixed swag and tails

Fixed swags are one of the more difficult soft furnishings to make, and are often left to the professionals. This method for a staggered pleat swag is foolproof as long as you measure accurately at each stage. A single swag can be made to fit a window as wide as 2m/2yd, but anything over 1m/1⅛yd becomes increasingly difficult to drape. To make two or even three overlapping swags for a wider window, simply use the chain method as described in step 1 to determine the size and overlap of the multiple swags.

you will need
- **curtain weight chain**
- **pale lining fabric, for the pattern**
- **pencil**
- **fabric**
- **lining fabric**
- **Velcro**
- **ruler**
- **sewing kit**

tip for formal fixed swag
Use a vertical work surface if possible to drape the chain to get a more accurate result.

making the swag pattern

For ease, the various measurements are identified by letters so record each measurement next to the appropriate letter. The "flat" measurement is the space along the top between the drapes of the swag, which can be varied depending on the effect you want. Radiating pleats, for example, all come from the same point and the "flat" measurement is the same length as the finished swag. In staggered pleats, shown here, the "flat" measurement is approximately half the finished length of the swag. Follow the instructions here using the diagram below for guidance.

A = half the width of the
flat measurement
plus 6cm/2½in
B = twice the depth of
the finished swag
C = three-quarters of B
D = half the length of
the chain

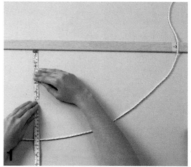
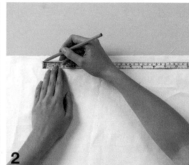

1 Mark the width of the swag on a wooden batten or insert pins into the back of the sofa. Drape a length of curtain weight chain between the marks so that the centre of the chain hangs down to one-fifth of the curtain length. Measure the length of the chain between the marks.

2 Cut a piece of pale lining fabric at least the length of the chain and twice the depth of the swag (two-fifths of the curtain drop). Fold in half crossways. Measuring from the fold, measure across to A and mark with a pencil.

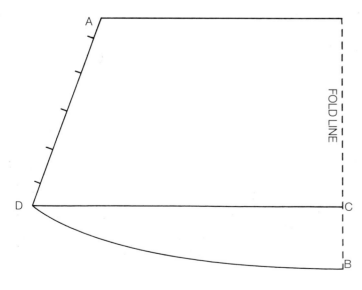

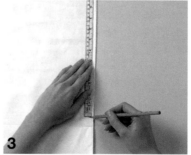
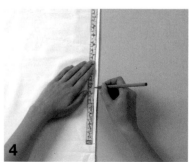

3 Measure twice the depth of the finished swag from the top edge of the fold and mark B.

4 Mark C, three-quarters of the way down the fold, and again several times across the template. Join the marks to draw a horizontal line.

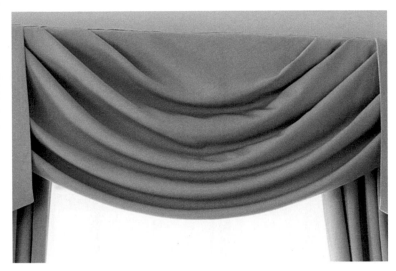

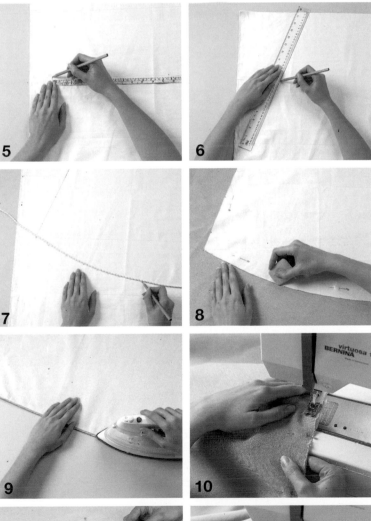

above *If you are making swags for the first time, choose a plain fabric so that you don't need to worry about matching the pattern.*

5 Measure along the horizontal line from the fold out to D, i.e. half the chain length measurement.

6 Draw a diagonal line between A and D. Measure this line and divide by either four or five to get a measurement of approximately 15–20cm/6–8in. Mark pleats along the diagonal line, beginning and ending with a half-measurement, e.g. 10cm, 20cm, 20cm, 20cm, 10cm (4in, 8in, 8in, 8in, 4in). These marks show where to fold the fabric for the pleats at each end of the swag.

7 Arrange the curtain weight chain between D and B until you get a soft curve that flattens out along the bottom towards the fold. Mark the line with a pencil.

8 Cut out the pattern and pin to the main fabric. Mark along the bottom edge and add 1.5cm/⅝in seam allowance on the other sides. This type of swag is usually cut on the cross, but stripes or boldly patterned fabrics are cut with the pattern centred and on the straight grain.

9 Using the same pattern, cut out the lining fabric. Pin to the main fabric, right sides facing. Stitch along the bottom edge, then trim to 5mm/¼in. Turn the swag through. Press, with the lining slightly to the inside along the bottom edge.

10 Pin along the top edge only of the swag. Stay-stitch, leaving a 1cm/½in seam allowance. Stay-stitch is simply a long machine stitch that secures the fabric temporarily until the seam is completed.

draping the swag

To drape the swag professionally, work along the edge of a padded work surface such as an ironing board or the back of a sofa.

11 Cut notches at each of the pleat marks. Pin the top edge of the swag to the work surface. Mark the centre and measure out each side half the uppermost swag width. Fold the swag along the top edge, at the first notch and pin at an angle, 6cm/2½in from the end. Pin the second pleat about half the pleat width along. Continue pinning the pleats; the last pleat should be in line with the half-swag mark.

12 Pin the second side. Adjust the pleats until you are happy with the angle and drape of the folds. Pin the pleats carefully then lift the swag off the work surface. Stay-stitch along the top edge to secure the pleats.

13 Trim the top edge level with the flat centre section. Cut a 13cm/5in strip of fabric, 3cm/1¼in longer than the width of the swag. Pin the strip along the right side and stitch. Press 1.5cm/⅝in along the top of the strip and fold over, right sides together. Stitch the ends, turn through and slip-stitch.

14 Pin a strip of loop Velcro along the top edge of the binding on the inside. Stitch down both sides. If tails are being added or two swags overlap, stitch hook Velcro to the other side of the binding where the pieces will overlap. Attach hook Velcro to the top front edge of the pelmet board and hang the swag.

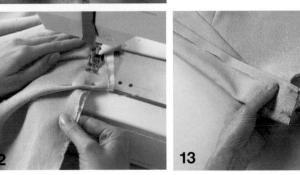

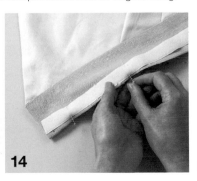

▷

formal fixed tails

Tails are much simpler to make than swags. The pattern is a standard size and can be kept and used again for other curtains. Tails are usually the same width regardless of the style of the curtain but vary in length, the longest coming halfway down the curtain. The inside short edge of the tail should be exactly the same length as the finished swag.

making the pattern for the formal tails

Cut out the lining fabric 122cm/48in wide and the required length of the finished tail. To make the medium-length tail shown here, measure one-third of the curtain length down one side of the lining fabric. Measure one-fifth of the curtain length down the other side and join the two marks with a pencil line (see below).

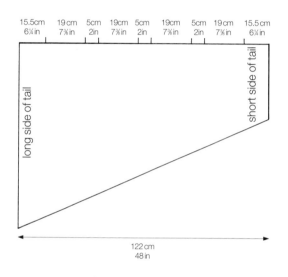

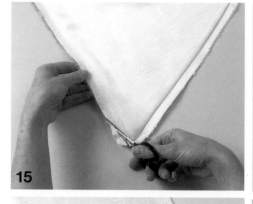

15

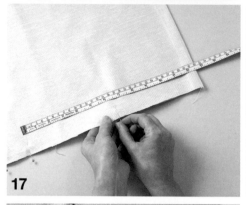

17

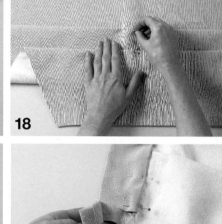

16

18

19   **20**

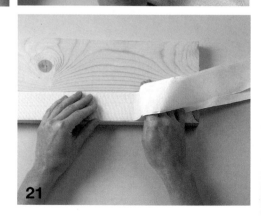

21

15 Place the pattern on the fabric, centring any pattern. Cut out, adding a 1.5cm/⅝in seam allowance all round. Turn the pattern over and cut a second tail to match. Cut two matching tails from contrast fabric. Pin each pair of fabric and lining right sides together, and stitch down the sides and along the bottom sloping edge. Trim the seams and the excess fabric at the points.

16 Press the seams flat, then turn the tails through. Roll the seams and press the edges from the lining side. Drop a curtain weight into the long point of each tail.

17 Measure along the top edge to mark the position of the pleats shown in the diagram, inserting pins at each point.

18 Beginning at the short tail edge, fold the first pleat. Pin it at the top and part way down the length. Pin the other pleats, checking that all the folds are parallel.

19 Cut a 13cm/5in strip of fabric the width of the pleated tail plus 6cm/2½in seam allowance. Cut off an 18.5cm/7¼in piece. Working along the top from the inside edge, pin the long strip to the tail, right sides together and raw edges aligned. Turn over the short edge of the strip. Press it level with the return mark – 15cm/6in from the outside edge. Fold over 1cm/½in on the second strip. Pin and stitch it along the remainder of the tail.

20 Press under 1.5cm/⅝in along the top and side edges of the binding. Cut a notch at the join between the strips. Fold the strips to the wrong side and slip stitch in place. Pin, then stitch a piece of loop Velcro along the underside of each section of the binding.

21 Stick hook Velcro along the top of the pelmet board, along the front edge and down each side. Staple to secure. Hang the tail on top of the swag, sticking it to the pelmet return and fitting the rest to the front edge.

stiffened tie-backs

Stiffened tie-backs are the most common way of holding back curtains. They are made from buckram, a stiffened hessian (burlap) that is lightweight, holds its shape well, and can be designed in a variety of shapes. Make several tie-back templates, marked with the size and the length of trimming required, and to try them on your curtains to help you decide the ideal shape.

you will need
- pencil and paper
- starched hessian (burlap) buckram
- interlining
- fabric
- flanged cord
- brass curtain rings
- sewing kit

tip for stiffened tie-backs
Piping can be used as an alternative to flanged cord.

1 Make a paper template and position it on the hessian (burlap) buckram, along the straight grain. Draw two shapes in pencil and cut out. Dampen the buckram by dipping it quickly into lukewarm water then place the shapes on interlining. Press with a hot iron to seal.

2 Allow the buckram to dry, then cut out the shapes in interlining, cutting close to the edge with no seam allowance.

3 Place one shape, interlining side down, on the wrong side of the fabric and draw along the top edge. Move the shape down about 5mm/¼in and draw round the remaining outline. Mark an accurate 1.5cm/⅝in seam allowance and cut out along this line. Cut four in total.

4 To make the front of each tie-back, cut a piece of cord to fit around the edge. Pin it to the right side of a fabric shape, beginning at the top edge and pinning it along the seamline. Snip into the flanged edge (cord tape) to allow the cord to bend around the corners.

5 Tack (baste) the flanged edge, close to the cord. Check that the tacking stitches follow the marked seamline on the wrong side. Flatten one end of the cord and oversew to the fabric.

6 Trim the other end of the cord to length and flatten it. Place it next to the oversewn end so that it looks like a piece of uncut cord. Tack both ends securely.

7 With right sides together, tack another shape to the front. Stitch round the edge, leaving a long gap at the bottom for inserting the buckram. Trim the seams to reduce bulk and notch the curves. Turn right side out.

8 Push the buckram inside, keeping the seam allowances to the back. Pull the lower edge to the reverse side and slip-stitch the backing fabric just inside the cord. Sew curtain rings on the back at each end.

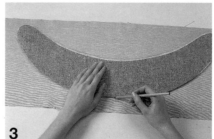

binding stiffened tie-backs

This alternative finish complements curtains with a contrast border down the leading edge of each curtain. The shape is slightly different, with a loop fastening instead of curtain rings, but the preparation is the same as for stiffened tie-backs.

you will need
- **starched hessian (burlap) buckram**
- **interlining**
- **fabric and contrast**
- **sewing kit**

tip for binding stiffened tie-backs
Add a matching border to the curtain for a co-ordinated look.

1 Follow the instructions for the stiffened tie-backs to cut the buckram and attach the interlining to the buckram and cut out. Draw along the top edge of the main fabric and move the template down about 5mm/¼in before completing the shape. Add 1.5cm/⅝in seam allowance to each end. For each tie-back, cut out two lining shapes, adding a seam allowance to all edges.

2 Using contrast fabric, cut sufficient 5cm/2in-wide bias strips to fit twice the length of each tie-back. With right sides together pin strips along the top and bottom edges of one fabric shape for each tie-back to make a binding and stitch in place.

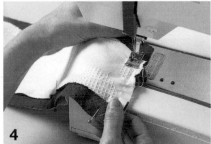

3 For the hanging loop, cut one strip of bias binding 8cm/3in long. Fold the long edges into the centre and press. Fold in half along the length to make a narrow strip, press and stitch along the edge. Form a loop and pin the short ends to one end of the tie-back, so that when it is folded back it faces up at the same angle as the tie-back. Make another for the other end. Make two for the other tie-back.

4 With right sides together, pin the lining fabric tie-back shape to the first shape. Stitch around the edge, leaving a large gap along the bottom.

5 Trim across the corners and turn through. Tuck the buckram inside, keeping the seam allowances to the back. Pin and slip-stitch the gap.

plait (braid) tie-backs

Use plaited (braided) tie backs to add a decorative feature to curtains. Tubes are made from rolls of wadding (batting) that are covered in fabric and stitched in one easy step. To see what the tie-back will look like, roll short lengths of wadding, cover them with fabric and plait them. Hold them up to the curtain and increase or decrease the wadding to suit your preference. Hold a tape measure around the curtain to find the required finished length.

you will need
- 100g/4oz wadding (batting)
- fabric to match curtains
- contrast fabric
- brass curtain rings or "D" rings
- sewing kit

tip for plait (braid) tie-backs
Use a soft fabric that doesn't crease easily for this tie-back.

1 Cut 1.5m/1⅝yd strips of wadding (batting) the required width and roll up fairly tightly. Stitch along the edge with long herringbone stitches to secure. Make three rolls for each tie-back.

2 Check the width of fabric required to cover each roll and add 2cm/¾in seam allowance all around. Cut three strips of fabric each 1.5m/1⅝yd long, with two strips in contrast fabric. Press under 1cm/½in down each long side.

3 Wrap a strip of fabric around a roll of wadding, leaving 1.5cm/⅝in of fabric above the short end of the wadding. Pin the fabric together at the top. Holding the edges together, stitch a little at a time until the wadding roll is covered in fabric. Repeat to make three tubes.

4 Keeping the seams along the top, pin the three rolls together at one end, with the contrast in the middle.

5 Cut out a 5 x 8cm/2 x 3in rectangle of fabric for each end of the tie-back. Pin the rectangle across the end of the strips, right sides together, and stitch 1.5cm/⅝in from the edge.

6 Fold in the outside edges of the fabric rectangle and pin. Turn down the top edge to bind the raw edges neatly. Hem securely.

7 Sew a curtain ring or "D" ring on to the binding on the inside, so that half the ring is jutting out.

8 Attach the ring to the tie-back hook or to a fixed point, using a piece of tape. Working from the right side, plait (braid) the rolls of fabric so that the seams remain on the underside. Measure the length of the plait, and trim to size if required. Finish the end of the tie-back with a rectangle of fabric and curtain "D" ring to match the other end.

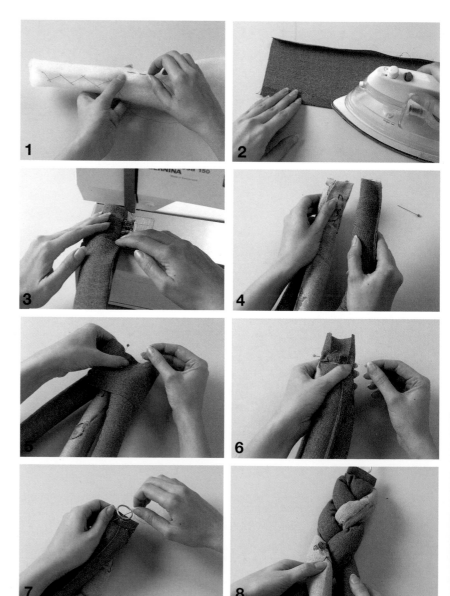

ruched tie-backs

Soft or sheer fabrics are ideal for this ruched tie-back. The effect is very delicate but the tie-back is quite sturdy as it has a stiffened interfacing inside. The softness comes from a layer of polyester wadding (batting), which supports the fabric and holds the ruching in place.

you will need

- fusible pelmet-weight interfacing
- 50g/2oz fabric-backed wadding (batting)
- lightweight fabric
- thin cord
- white "D" rings
- sewing kit

tip for ruched tie-backs

If more fullness is required there can be less ruching on what will be the back of the tie-back.

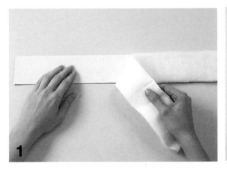

1 Decide on the length and width of the tie-back. Cut out a rectangle of fusible pelmet-weight interfacing and fabric-backed wadding (batting) for each tie-back. Place the wadding on the interfacing, turn them over and press gently with a steam iron to fuse the layers together.

2 Cut a strip of fabric three to four times the length and twice as wide as the tie-back, plus 1cm/½in seam allowances. Fold in half lengthways, with right sides together, and stitch a 5mm/¼in seam. Turn through the tube of fabric to the right side.

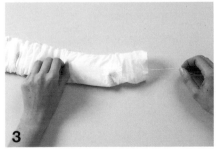

3 Stitch a length of thin cord on to one end of the interfacing. Feed the cord through the tube and hold it while gently pulling the fabric back along the interfacing. For the binding, cut a piece of double-thickness fabric 5 x 8cm/2 x 3in for each end of the ruched tie-back.

4 Pin across the end of the strip, right sides together, and stitch 1.5cm/⅝in from the edge. Fold in the outside edges and pin. Turn down the top edge to bind the raw edges. Hem the ends.

5 Adjust the gathers evenly along the length. Stitch a "D" ring to each end so that the ring juts out halfway.

pleated tie-backs

This elegant tie-back is another version of the stiffened tie-back, and uses binding to secure the pleats. It works best with crisp fabrics that can be pressed to hold a crease. You will need about ½m/½yd of fabric to make the pleated section for two tie-backs.

you will need

- **fabric**
- **iron-on interfacing**
- **pencil or tailor's chalk**
- **starched hessian (burlap) buckram**
- **"D" rings**
- **sewing kit**

tip for pleated tie-backs
Make sure the print is facing in the right direction before cutting the template shape.

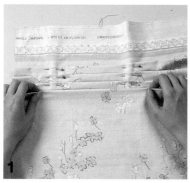
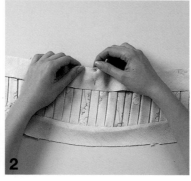
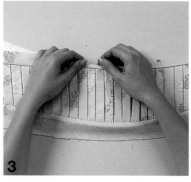
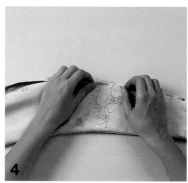

1 Fold the fabric into pleats of the size required. Measure the first few, about 1–2cm/½–¾in, then pleat the rest by eye if you feel sufficiently confident. Pin the pleats in several places along the length. Continue until you have sufficient pleated fabric for both tie-backs. Press the pleats, then stitch along the top and bottom edges and remove the pins. Support the pleats by pressing iron-on interfacing on the wrong side. Draw around your chosen tie-back template. Cut one shape for each tie-back in buckram and pleated fabric, adding seam allowances to the short ends only. Cut the backing fabric with seam allowances all round.

2 Cut 5cm/2in-wide bias strips of fabric for the top and bottom of each tie-back. With right sides together, pin and stitch along the top and bottom of the pleated shape.

3 Lay the pleated fabric over the interlined buckram. Fold the binding over to the reverse side and pin.

4 Press under the edges of the backing fabric shape and slip-stitch on to the reverse side of the tie-back, covering the raw edges of the binding. Sew a "D" ring to each inside end of the tie-back.

hold-backs

Hold-backs are an alternative way of holding a curtain to one side, although here they can be used to hold the fabric of the draped swag in place. They are available in a wide variety of shapes, often designed to match the finials on the end of curtain poles. This hold-back is rather like a covered button. The front disc (part of a kit) is covered with a circle of fabric, fitted to a thin stem and then screwed to the wall.

you will need
- **pencil**
- **self-cover hold-back kit**
- **fabric**
- **strong sewing thread**
- **wadding (batting)**
- **double-sided tape**
- **sewing kit**

tip for hold-backs

If the curtains or swag are patterned, make the hold-back in plain fabric.

1 Draw around the front of the hold-back on the fabric and cut out a circle 2.5cm/1in larger all around.

2 Work a line of running stitch around the edge of the circle, using a length of strong thread.

3 Cut a circle of wadding (batting) to fit over the front of the hold-back and stick in place with double-sided tape.

4 Place the hold-back disc face down on the fabric and pull up the threads around it. Sew in the ends securely. Assemble and fix the hold-back in place following the manufacturer's instructions.

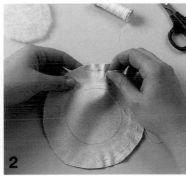

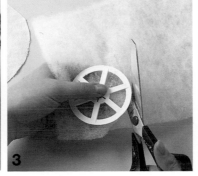

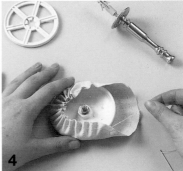

sheer curtain with heading tape

Sheer curtains are made in much the same way as ordinary curtains, although they are often left closed, to screen the sunlight or to provide privacy. Special lightweight tapes are available for sheer curtains, and are less conspicuous from the right side as they let the light through. If curtains remain closed all the time, there is no need for a curtain rail and the curtain can simply be attached to a strip of Velcro stuck along the top of the window frame. Sheer curtains do not normally have side hems or seams as the selvage is not conspicuous and hangs better than a stitched edge. Simply turn up the hem and attach the heading tape.

you will need
- **sheer fabric**
- **Velcro heading tape for sheer fabric**
- **sewing kit**

tip for sheer curtain with heading tape
Specialized Velcro heading tape is available in a variety of widths especially for this purpose.

1 Trim the fabric along a straight thread. Turn under an accurate double 5cm/2in hem along the bottom edge of the fabric and press.

2 Lift the fabric carefully on to the sewing machine and stitch the hem. Avoid using pins in case they mark the delicate fabric.

3 Cut the curtain to length and press the seam allowance to the wrong side. Pull the cords out at one end of the heading tape and fold the end over. Pin the tape just below the top of the curtain.

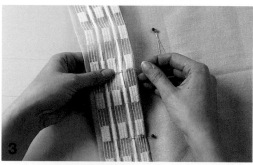

4 Fold the other end of the tape under and stitch the end. Stitch each long side of the tape, working both in the same direction.

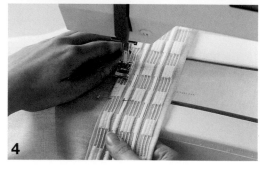

sheer flat curtain

This sheer flat curtain has less fullness in it than the sheer curtain made with a heading tape, and looks attractive with deep hems on all sides and mitred corners. Allow 1–1½ times the track length.

you will need

- **sheer fabric**
- **curtain clips**
- **sewing kit**

1 For a curtain with mitred corners, it is essential to straighten the fabric before cutting it. Pull a thread across one end of the fabric then cut along the line.

2 Press under a double 6cm/2⅜in hem along all edges, checking that the corners are absolutely square. Open out the hems and fold over each corner so that the point is level with the inside creases. Trim across the diagonal line.

3 Fold up the hems again, as for a double mitre (see basic techniques) and pin. Check that the corner comes to a neat point and that the edges of the mitre seams are level.

4 Tack (baste) the hem and mitred corners carefully, then stitch close to the inside edge. Slip-stitch the mitred corner and remove the tacking threads. To hang the curtains, space curtain clips evenly along the top of each curtain every 10–15cm/4–6in.

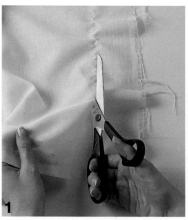

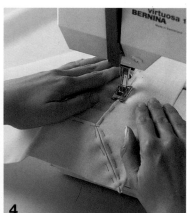

tied-up blind

This simple blind is perfect for a tall window where it is left tied-up all the time, rather than being continually let up and down. To make it easier to raise and lower, or to create a slightly different look, it can be fitted with a dowel along the bottom edge, rather like a reverse roller blind.

you will need

- **lightweight fabric**
- **5cm/2in-wide ribbon**
- **Velcro**
- **sewing kit**
  for hanging the blind
- **screw-eyes**
- **2.5 x 5cm/1 x 2in wooden batten, the width of the blind**
- **fixing brackets and screws**

tip for tied-up blind
To hang the blind see page 21.

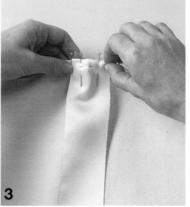
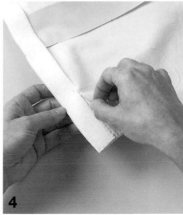

1 Cut two pieces of fabric the required size of the finished blind, plus 3cm/1¼in seam allowance all around. Place the two pieces right sides together and raw edges aligned and stitch all around, leaving a gap along the top edge. Trim the corners and turn through.

2 Ease out the corners and press the edges. Slip-stitch the gap closed along the top edge and press. Cut two lengths of ribbon, each twice the length of the blind plus 20cm/8 in for tying.

3 Find the middle of each ribbon and position it so that the midpoint sits at the top of the blind, approximately quarter of the way across from each side edge. Pin and tack (baste) in position so that half the ribbon falls down the back of the blind and half down the front.

4 Pin a piece of loop Velcro along the top edge of the blind on the wrong side. Stitch the top edge of the Velcro, then slip-hem the lower edge, stitching through the backing fabric only. Tie the ribbons in bows, looping up the fabric.

reefer blind

With its thick rope and eyelets, a reefer blind has a distinctly nautical feel and is ideal for a bathroom or kitchen. There must be an odd number of eyelets so that the rope comes from the wrong side at the top and finishes in a decorative knot on the right side at the bottom. You will need four times the length and twice the width of cord. The eyelets and screw-eye fittings should be large enough to allow the rope to slide through easily.

you will need

- **fabric**
- **contrast fabric**
- **lining fabric**
- **Velcro**
- **hammer**
- **eyelet tool**
- **embroidery scissors (optional)**
- **1–1.5cm/½–⅝ in eyelets**
- **rope or thick cord**
- **sewing kit**

for hanging the blind

- **screw-eyes**
- **2.5 x 5cm/1 x 2in wooden batten, the width of the blind**
- **fixing brackets and screws**

tip for reefer blind
To hang the blind see page 21.

1 Cut out the main fabric 21cm/8½in less than the required width, adding 5cm/2in seam allowance to the length. Cut two strips of contrast fabric each 18cm/7in wide to fit down the sides of the blind. With right sides together, stitch the borders to the main fabric. Press the seams open.

2 Cut a piece of lining fabric 9cm/3½in narrower than the finished blind, adding 3cm/1¼in seam allowance to the length. With right sides together, stitch the lining to the blind

down the side seams and press the seams open. Centre the lining between the borders and pin along the bottom edge. Stitch, turn through, then ease out the corners and press.

3 Press under 2.5cm/1in along the top edge of the lining and main fabric. Pin loop Velcro along this top edge, covering the raw edges. Stitch the top edge of the Velcro, though all the layers, then slip-hem the lower edge to the lining only.

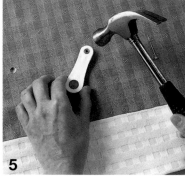

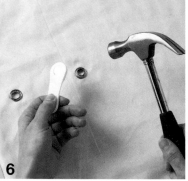

4 Mark the position of the eyelets, 10cm/4in from the border edge. They should be about 10cm/4in apart, with the last eyelets 5cm/2in from the bottom of the blind. Adjust the spacing to get an odd number.

5 Using a hammer and eyelet tool, cut a hole at each mark. If the fabric is too thick to cut through, cut around the indent with embroidery scissors.

6 Turn over the blind. Insert the tube part of each eyelet from the right side, then fit the ring over the top. Work on a solid surface so that you can hammer the eyelets in place more easily.

7 Thread a length of rope or cord through each row of eyelets, starting from the lining side at the top. Tie the end in a knot on the right side.

Roman blind

This is an elegant, tailored way to dress a window. It is a fabric panel with wooden dowels fitted into casings across the back, which pull up to make neat pleats as the blind is raised. A Roman blind is most successful made in crisp, firmly woven furnishing fabric, but it can also look stunning if it is made in sheer fabric with a solid, contrasting border.

calculating the fabric

Measure the required finished size of the blind and add 10cm/4in to both the length and width for seam allowances. The lining is the width and length of the finished blind, plus 6cm/2½in for each casing added to the length. The nylon cord is four times the length of the blind plus twice the width.

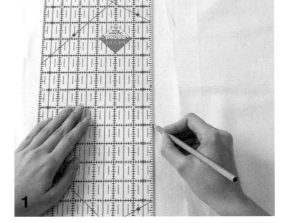

you will need

- **firmly woven furnishing fabric**
- **lining fabric**
- **pencil**
- **quilter's ruler (optional)**
- **Velcro**
- **7mm/⁵⁄₁₆ in-wide wooden dowel**
- **3mm x 2.5cm/⅛ x 1in wood lath**
- **small plastic rings (2 for each casing)**
- **nylon cord**
- **sewing kit**

for hanging the blind

- **screw-eyes**
- **2.5 x 5cm/1 x 2in wooden batten, the width of the blind**
- **fixing brackets and screws**

◻ **tip for Roman blind**
To hang the blind see page 21.

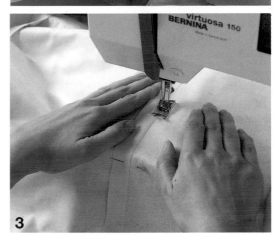

1 Cut out the main fabric and lining. Draw a pencil line horizontally across the lining fabric, 25cm/10in from the bottom edge. Mark a casing line 6cm/2½in above it. Continue marking the lines and casing lines 25cm/10 in apart. A quilter's rule is ideal for accurate marking.

2 Press under a 2.5cm/1in turning down both side edges of the lining. With wrong sides together, fold the lining, pinning each pencil line to the casing line above it. Stitch along the pinned line, reverse-stitching at each end for strength. Press the casing to one side.

3 Press under 5cm/2in down both sides of the main fabric. Pin the lining in the centre on the reverse side of the fabric. Stitch on top of the previous casing stitches, reverse-stitching at each end.

▷

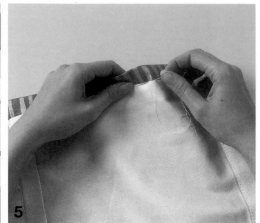

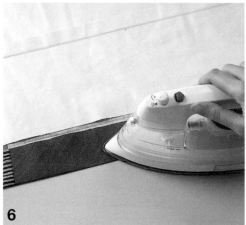

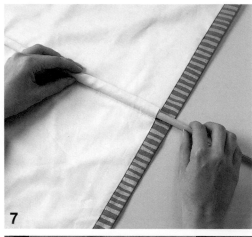

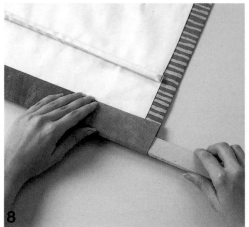

4 Turn over 2cm/¾in along the top edge and pin a strip of loop Velcro on top. Stitch along the top edge of the Velcro, then slip-hem the lower edge to the lining fabric only.

5 Slip-hem the side seams of the lining, taking care not to stitch through to the right side.

6 Trim the lining 8cm/3in from the bottom edge. Turn up and press a double 4cm/1½in hem along the bottom edge of the blind. Hem the blind, stitching into the lining only.

7 Cut the dowel 2cm/¾in shorter than the casing length. Insert one through each casing, then stitch the ends.

8 Cut the wooden lath 2cm/¾in shorter than the blind width. Slot it through the bottom hem, then stitch the ends.

9 Hand sew two plastic rings on to each casing, each one 10cm/4in in from each side. Cut the nylon cord in half. Thread one end of the first piece of cord down through one set of rings, and tie it securely to the last ring. Repeat with the other piece of cord.

below *Vertical stripes are an ideal choice for the simple folds of Roman blinds.*

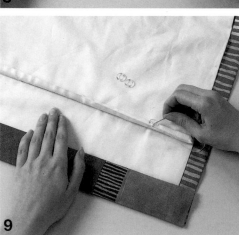

London blind

A London blind is flat along the top edge, but has inverted box pleats down each side. The blind looks effective made in a vertically striped fabric, with the pleats opening to reveal an interesting colour or pattern as the blind is pulled up. The amounts of fabric quoted below include some flexibility so that you can make the best use of the fabric. Bear in mind that if the pleats begin approximately 15cm/6in from the side edge of the blind, the centre of each pleat will be twice that distance, i.e. 30cm/12in, from the side edge.

above *Arrange the folds neatly once the blind is pulled up.*

calculating the fabric

The main fabric is cut 13cm/5in wider than the batten width, with another 61cm/24in added to the width for the pleats. Add 4cm/1½in to the length for seam allowances. The lining is the same length and 7cm/2¾in narrower.

Take a tape measure with you when you are buying the fabric, and choose one that can be folded down a stripe or that will show a pattern inside a pleat.

For each length of cord used, allow twice the length plus one width.

you will need

- **fabric**
- **lining fabric**
- **Velcro**
- **small plastic rings**
- **nylon cord**
- **sewing kit**
- *for hanging the blind*
- **screw-eyes**
- **2.5 x 5cm/1 x 2in wooden batten, the width of the blind**
- **fixing brackets and screws**

1 Cut out the main fabric and lining fabric. Pin right sides together, and stitch the side seams. Press the seams open and centre the lining on the main fabric. Stitch along the bottom edge and turn through. Press the edges.

2 To mark the position of the pleats, insert a pin 15cm/6in in from the side seam and another two pins each 15cm/6in apart. With pins mark a pleat to match on the other side.

3 Matching the outside pins, fold the blind right sides together and measure 20cm/8in from the top edge. Tack (baste) and stitch the pleat seams, reverse-stitching at each end.

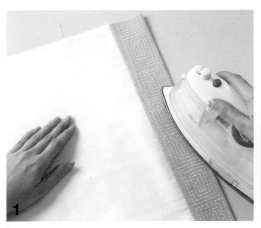

1

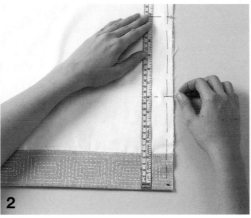

2

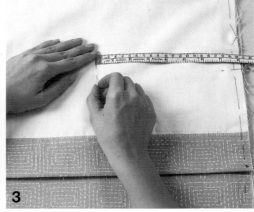

3

▷

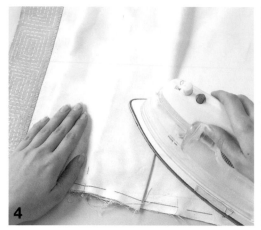

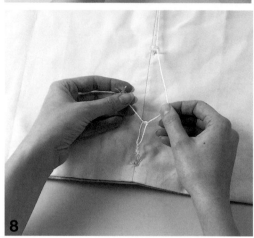

4 Open out the pleats to form inverted box pleats and tack (baste) along the top edge. Pin the pleats from the right side and press. Press again on the wrong side.

5 Fold over a 2cm/¾in turning across the top of the blind and press. Stitch a length of Velcro tape along the top edge. Slip-hem the lower edge of the Velcro to the lining only.

6 Hand stitch a small plastic ring in the centre of each pleat on the lining side, 5cm/2in from the bottom edge. Repeat every 10–13cm/4–5in all the way up the blind.

7 Cut two equal lengths of nylon cord and thread one through each row of rings.

8 Tie the end of each cord securely to the bottom ring.

tips for London blind

To hang the blind see page 21.

Pin the pleats in position before pulling the blind up for the first time.

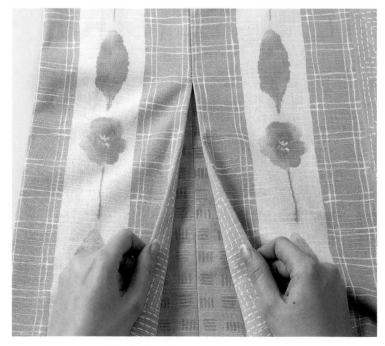

above *If the fabric isn't wide enough and needs to be joined, position the seam down the centre of the pleats.*

above *Where possible, create the pleats so that an attractive motif shows when the blind is pulled up.*

Austrian blind

An Austrian blind is gathered across the top edge with heading tape, which allows the fabric to fall into soft, scalloped folds when the blind is raised. It looks rather like a curtain when it is let down. Its soft appearance lends itself to frills or fringing, which can be added down the sides as well as along the bottom, as here. Choose a soft, bouncy fabric that resists creasing.

calculating the fabric

Measure the track width and blind drop to the top of the frill. Allow 2–2½ times fullness across the width adding 3cm/1¼in for side hems. Add 5cm/2in to the blind drop for the length. See step 1 for the frill. For each length of cord used allow twice the length plus one width.

☐ **tip for** Austrian blind
To hang the blind see page 21.

you will need

- **fabric**
- **lining fabric**
- **Austrian blind tape**
- **8cm/3in-wide pencil pleat heading tape**
- **nylon cord**
- **sewing kit**

for hanging the blind:
- **screw-eyes**
- **Austrian blind rail or curtain track and 2.5 x 5cm/1 x 2in wooden batten, the width of the blind**

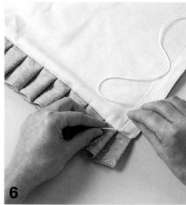

1 Cut out the main fabric and lining. For the pleated frill along the bottom edge of the blind, cut a strip of main fabric 13cm/5in wide and at least twice as long as the width of the blind. Press under 1cm/½in at each end to the wrong side and fold in half lengthways.

2 Place the strip along the bottom edge of the main fabric and 1.5cm/⅝in in from one side edge. Pin the strip into small pleats, about 1–2cm/½–¾in deep. Measure the first few pleats then work by eye until the pleats go all the way across the fabric, stopping 1.5cm/⅝in from the side edge.

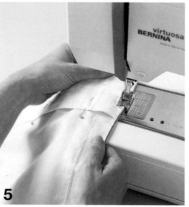

3 With right sides together, pin the lining fabric over the top of the pleats. Stitch down the sides of the blind and across the bottom. Trim across the corners, turn through and press. Pin a length of Austrian blind tape down each side of the blind. Space further lengths 50–60cm/20–24in apart.

4 Stitch the Austrian blind tape to the blind, stitching both sides of the tape in the same direction. Fill the spool with a thread colour that matches the main fabric and use a top thread to match the lining.

5 Fold over a 2cm/¾in turning across the top of the blind and press. Pin a length of pencil pleat heading tape 5mm/¼in from the top edge and stitch round all sides, leaving the tape cords free at one side.

6 Thread a length of nylon cord down each Austrian blind tape, going through a loop every 10–13cm/4–5in. Tie the cords securely to the last loop. Hang the blind from a special Austrian blind rail, or alternatively fit a wooden batten with screw-eyes behind a curtain track.

roller blind

Roller blind kits are available from department stores, and contain everything except the fabric. Ready-stiffened fabric for roller blinds is available, but if you want to use your choice of fabric it will need to be straightened, then sprayed with fabric stiffener before cutting to size. Avoid heavyweight or loosely woven fabric. Home-made roller blinds are suited to small or medium-size windows that require just one width of fabric.

measuring up for the blind kit

If the blind is to fit inside a recess, measure the exact width with a metal tape and deduct 3cm/1¼in for the blind mechanism. If it is to hang outside the window, add an extra 5cm /2in to each side of the recess so that it will completely cover the space. Buy a roller blind kit the exact width if possible, or get a longer one and cut it to length.

calculating the fabric

The width of the blind is the length of the roller, allowing for the end fixtures. There is no allowance for side seams as the stiffened fabric will not fray. Add 30cm/12in hem and roller allowance to the length. If the blind is to finish below the windowsill, add on another 5cm/2in.

you will need

- **closely woven furnishing fabric**
- **fabric stiffener spray**
- **quilter's ruler (optional)**
- **rotary cutter (optional)**
- **roller blind kit**
- **pencil**
- **long ruler**
- **double-sided tape**
- **sewing kit**

tip for roller blind
Always cut the fabric after spraying as it may shrink considerably.

1 Pull a thread at one end of the fabric and cut along the line to get the straight grain. Fold the fabric in half lengthways. If the corners don't meet exactly, straighten the fabric by pulling it on the diagonal or pinning selvage to selvage with the cut edges aligned and steam pressing it. Press the fabric. Following the manufacturer's instructions, spray it lightly with fabric stiffener horizontally and vertically on both sides to achieve a complete and even coverage.

2 Leave the fabric to dry, then press it, and cut to size. A quilter's ruler and rotary cutter are the ideal method to get square corners and straight edges with minimal handling of the fabric. Trim off the selvages and align the markings on the ruler with the cut edge. Cut across at right angles to the correct length.

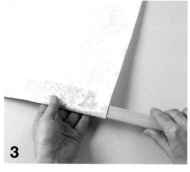  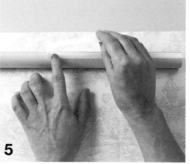 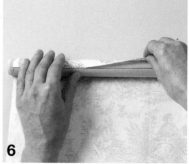

3 Fold over and press a double 4cm/1½in hem along the bottom edge. Stitch. Cut the wooden lath in the blind kit 2cm/¾in shorter than the finished width of the blind and slot it through the hem. Stitch the ends of the hem to secure. If a cord-holder is included in the kit, attach it in the centre of the lath on the right side.

4 Cut the roller 3cm/1¼in narrower than required to allow for the blind mechanism. So that the blind will roll straight, it is essential to mark a straight line down the centre of the roller, using a pencil and long ruler.

5 Stick a length of double-sided tape along the pencil line and then peel off the protective backing paper.

6 Place the roller across the wrong side of the fabric, 2–3cm/¾–1¼in from the top. Check that it is in the centre then stick the top edge of the fabric to the double-sided tape exactly along the marked line. Attach the spring mechanism and fitments to the ends of the roller. Attach the brackets to the recess or wall, and fit the blind according to the manufacturer's instructions.

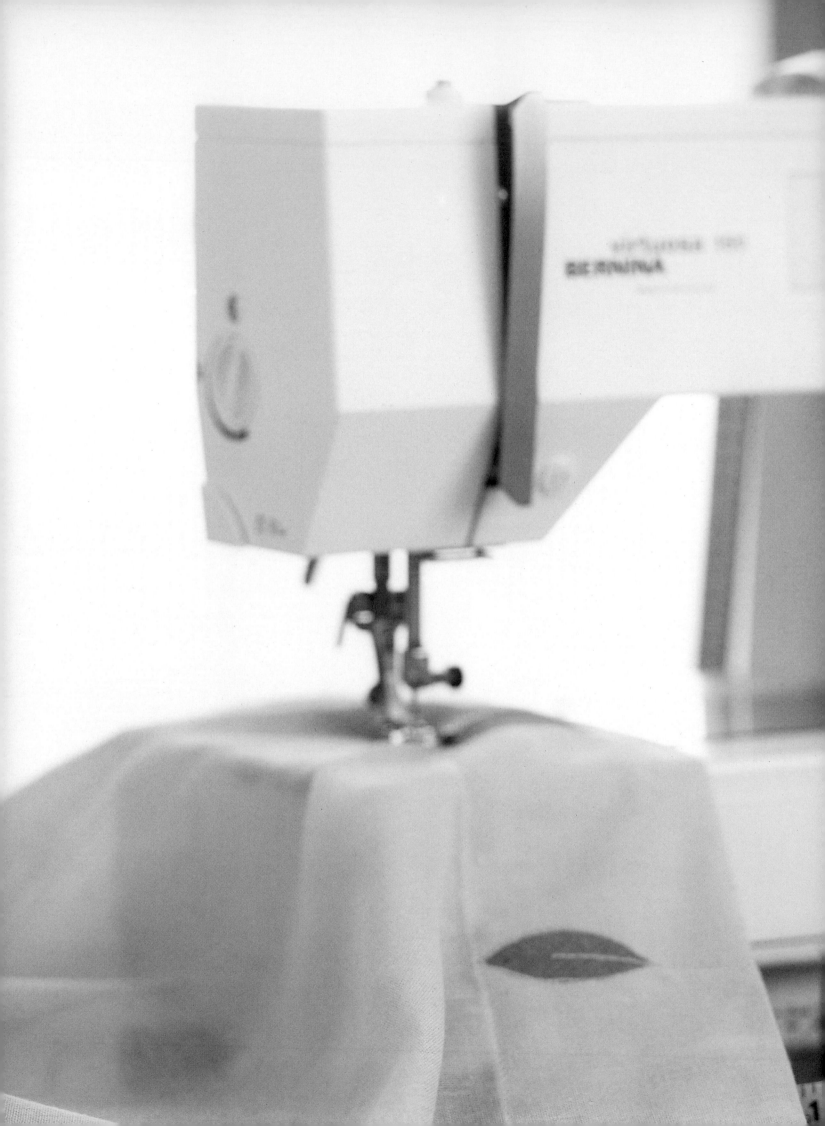

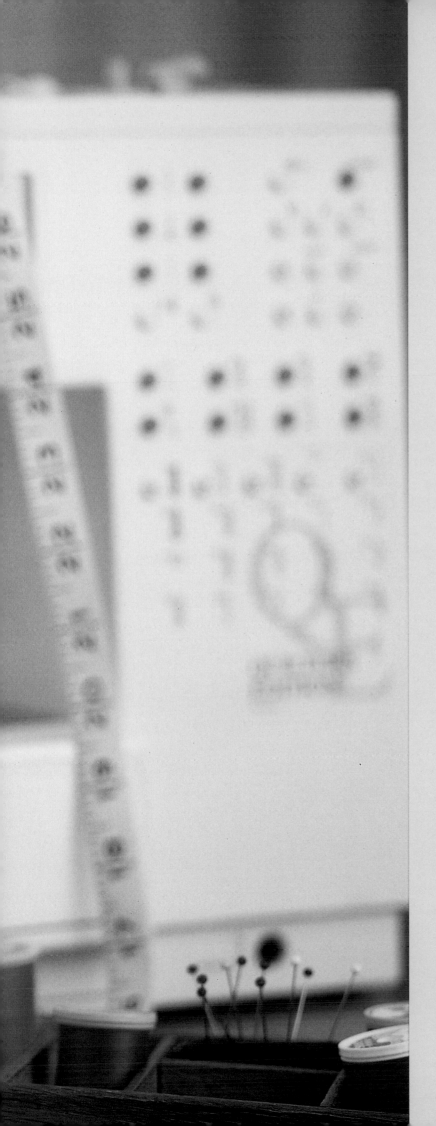

basic techniques

Technique makes the difference between something that looks average and something that looks immaculately tailored, with a crisp, professional finish. Take time to learn the basic techniques in the following pages – they will help you achieve perfect results that you can be proud of.

the sewing kit

You will probably have much of this equipment already in your sewing box. Check that the scissors you use for cutting fabric are perfectly sharp and do not use them for any other purpose.

1 Bodkin
Used to thread elastic, cord or ribbon through casings.

2 Dressmaker's carbon and tracing wheel
Used together to transfer markings to the wrong side of the fabric. Select carbon paper that is close in colour to the fabric colour but still visible. Always use white carbon paper on white fabric (it shows as a dull line).

3 Fabric markers
A pencil is suitable for marking most hard-surfaced fabrics and can be brushed off with a stiff brush. A vanishing-ink pen will wash out in water or fade. Use a tracing pen to draw a design on waxed paper and then transfer it to the fabric by ironing over it.

4 Fusible bonding web
This glue mesh is used to stick two layers of fabric together. It is available in various widths. The narrow bands shown here are useful for heavyweight hems and facings, and the wider widths are used for appliqué.

5 Hand-sewing needles
"Sharps" (medium-length, all-purpose needles) are used for general hand sewing. For fine hand sewing, use the shorter, round-eyed "betweens". Hand-sewing needles are numbered from 1–10, with 10 being the finest.

6 Pincushion
Useful for holding pins and needles as you work.

7 Dressmaker's pins
Use normal household pins for most sewing, and lace pins for delicate fabrics. Glass-headed pins are easy to see.

8 Quilter's tape
Used to mark very accurate seam allowances. The tape is 5mm/¼in wide but can be placed further from the raw edge to stitch wider seams.

9 Rouleau turner
A metal tool used to turn through rouleau loops.

10 Safety pins
Use to hold thick layers of fabric together.

11 Scissors
You will need a large pair of drop-handle (bent-handle) scissors for cutting out fabric, a medium pair for trimming seams or cutting small pieces of fabric, and a small pair of sharp, pointed embroidery scissors for cutting threads and snipping into curves. Never cut paper with sewing scissors as it dulls the blade.

12 Seam ripper
A small cutting tool for undoing machine-stitching mistakes. Also useful for cutting buttonholes.

13 Tape measure
Buy a 150cm/60in tape with metal tips in a material such as fibreglass that will not stretch. A small metal ruler with an adjustable guide is useful when pinning hems, tucks and buttonholes.

14 Tailor's chalk
Used to mark fabric. Keep the edge sharp by shaving it with medium scissors. Test on the right side of the fabric to ensure it will brush off.

15 Thimble
Worn on the middle finger of your sewing hand to prevent accidental needle pricks when hand sewing.

16 Sewing threads
For best results, choose a thread that matches the fibre content of the fabric. Use a shade of thread that matches the fabric. If there is no match go one shade darker. Use strong thread for furnishing fabrics and for hand quilting. Tacking (basting) thread is cheaper and poorer-quality. Use strong buttonhole twist or linen thread for buttonholes.

17 Tissue paper
When machine stitching delicate fabrics, tack (baste) strips of tissue paper to each side of the seam and stitch as normal. Tear the tissue paper off afterwards.

the sewing machine

For soft furnishings, a sturdy flat-bed sewing machine is the most suitable kind but any ordinary domestic machine can be used.

Balance wheel
This controls the sewing machine. On manual machines, turn the wheel to lower the needle.

Bobbin winder
This allows you to fill the bobbin quickly and evenly.

Foot control or knee control
This starts, stops and controls the speed at which the machine stitches.

Needle clamp
This secures the shaft of the needle into the machine.

Needle plate
The needle plate surrounds the feed teeth and has a hole for the needle.

Presser foot
This holds the fabric flat on the needle plate so that a stitch can form.

Stitch length control
Use this to alter the length of straight stitches and the density of zigzag stitch.

Stitch width control
This controls the amount the needle moves sideways. Use a suitable presser foot so that the needle doesn't break as it swings from side to side.

Thread take-up lever
This feeds the correct amount of thread from the spool down through to the needle.

Tension regulating dial
The tension dial alters the tension on the top thread.

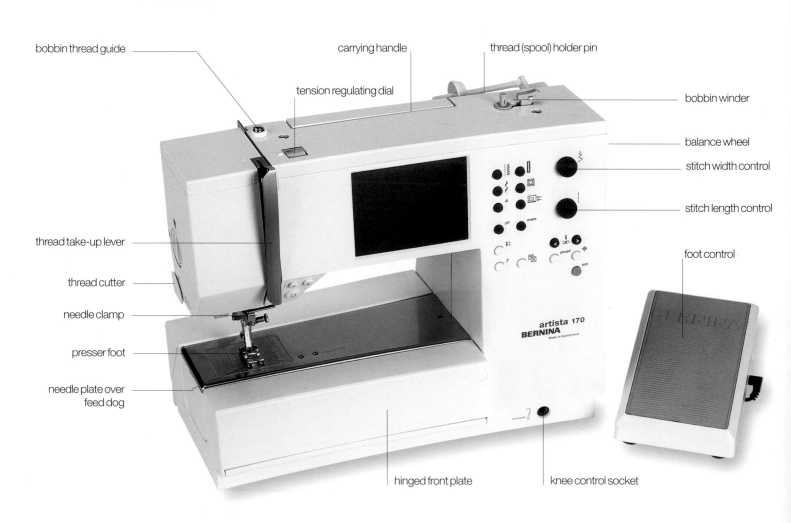

bobbin thread guide

carrying handle

thread (spool) holder pin

tension regulating dial

bobbin winder

balance wheel

stitch width control

stitch length control

thread take-up lever

thread cutter

needle clamp

presser foot

foot control

needle plate over feed dog

artista 170
BERNINA
Made in Switzerland

hinged front plate

knee control socket

Thread cutter

This is situated at the back of the sewing machine for cutting threads.

Thread (spool) holder pin

This holds the reel (spool) of thread when filling the bobbin and stitching.

MACHINE NEEDLES

Always select a machine needle to suit the fabric and the thread you are using; this will reduce the possibility of the needle breaking.

Universal needles

Universal sewing machine needles range in size from 70/9, used for fine fabrics, to 110/18, used for heavyweight fabrics. Size 80/12 is ideal for a mediumweight fabric. Keep a selection of needles to hand and change the needle when using a different weight of fabric. A fine needle will break if the fabric is too thick, and a large needle will damage a fine fabric.

Embroidery needles

These needles have larger eyes than normal to accommodate a wide range of decorative threads (floss). Keep a separate needle for each type of thread because the thread creates a groove on the needle that will cause other threads to break.

Top-stitch and jean-point needles

Special top-stitch needles have a very large eye to accommodate a thicker thread, although top stitching can also be worked using the same thread as the main fabric. Jean-point needles have a specially elongated sharp point to stitch through heavyweight fabrics.

Fitting the needle

Machine needles can only be fitted one way as they have a flat surface down one side (the shank) and a long groove down the other side (the shaft). When the needle is inserted, this groove should line up directly with the last thread guide. When the machine is in use, the thread runs down the groove and scores a unique channel into the metal. So when you change thread, you should change your needle, too.

zipper foot   clear-view foot   general all-purpose foot   buttonhole foot

MACHINE FEET

All sewing machines have interchangeable feet for different types of sewing. These are designed for particular functions such as stitching close to a zipper or piping cord. The most common ones are illustrated here, but you can buy other specialist (specialty) feet.

General-purpose foot The basic metal general-purpose foot is used for all general straight and zigzag stitching on ordinary fabrics.

Clear-view foot Similar to the general-purpose foot, this foot allows you to see where you are stitching. It can be cut away or made from clear plastic. Use for machine quilting or appliqué.

Zipper foot This allows you to stitch close to the zipper teeth, and to piping cord. On some, the needle can be adjusted to sew on either side. A special zipper foot is available for invisible zippers.

Buttonhole foot This foot has a metal strip to guide rows of satin stitch forwards and backwards, leaving a tiny gap between for cutting the buttonhole.

STITCH TENSION

A new sewing machine should have the tension correctly set, with the dial at the marked centre point. Try out any stitches you intend to use on a sample of the fabric.

To check the tension, bring all the pattern and zigzag dials back to zero and set the stitch length between 2 and 3 for normal stitching. Place a folded strip of fabric on the needle plate, lower the needle into the fabric and sew a row of straight stitches. These should look exactly the same on both sides.

Altering the tension

To tighten the tension, turn the dial towards the lower numbers; to loosen it, turn towards the higher numbers. This will automatically affect the tension of the thread coming through the bobbin case. If the top tension dial is far from the centre, the spring on the bobbin case is probably wrong.

Only alter the lower tension as a last resort. You should be able to dangle the bobbin case without the thread slipping through. Shake the thread and the bobbin case should drop a little. Turn the screw on the side of the bobbin case slightly to alter the tension. Test the stitching again on a sample of fabric and alter the top tension this time until the stitches are perfect.

maintenance and trouble-shooting

Like a car, a sewing machine will only run well if it is used frequently and looked after. Cleaning is essential when you change fabrics, especially from a dark to a light-coloured one. Remove the sewing machine needle. Use a stiff brush to clean out the fluff (lint) along the route the top thread takes through the machine. Unscrew the needle plate and brush out any fluff from around the feed teeth. Remove the bobbin case to check that no thread is trapped in the mechanism.

above *Immaculately-tailored seams will ensure your soft furnishing items last longer as well as look better.*

Oil the machine from time to time, following the instructions in your handbook. Only use a couple of drops of oil. Leave the machine overnight with a fabric pad beneath the presser foot, then wipe the needle before use. Some new machines are self-lubricating. Even if you take good care of your machine, problems can occur. Some of the more common problems are listed below.

The machine works too slowly

The machine may have two speeds and may be set on slow. More likely, it hasn't been used for a while and oil could be clogging the working parts. Run the machine without a needle for a minute to loosen all the joints. Check that the foot control is not obstructed. As a last resort, ask a dealer to check the tension belt.

No stitches form

Ensure that the bobbin is full and inserted correctly. Check that the needle is facing in the right direction and threaded from the grooved side.

The needle doesn't move

Check first of all that the balance wheel is tight and that the bobbin winder is switched off. If the needle still doesn't move, the problem may be caused by thread trapped in the sewing hook behind the bobbin case. Remove the bobbin case and take hold of the thread end. Rock the balance wheel backwards and forwards until the thread comes out.

left *A professional look to soft furnishings is a result of seams stitched with perfect tension and no puckers.*

The machine jams

Rock, but don't force, the balance wheel gently to loosen the threads and take the fabric out. Remove the needle, unscrew the needle plate and brush out any fluff (lint). Alternatively, check that the machine is correctly threaded and that the fabric is far enough under the presser foot when you begin stitching.

The needle bends or breaks

A needle will break if it hits the foot, bobbin case or needle plate. Check that you are using the correct foot. When using a zipper foot, a common mistake is forgetting to move the needle to the left or right for straight or zigzag-stitching. Check the bobbin case is inserted properly. Make sure the take-up lever is at its highest point before fitting.

A needle that has been bent will break if it hits the needle plate. To avoid bent needles, sew slowly over pins and thick seams. A needle will also bend if there is a knot in the thread, or if the fabric is pulled through the machine faster than the machine is sewing. Replace bent needles immediately.

The fabric does not feed through

This can happen when the feed teeth are lowered in the darning or machine embroidery position. Close zigzag or embroidery stitches will bunch up in the general-purpose foot, so change the foot to one that is cut away underneath to allow the stitches to feed through. Check also that the machine is correctly threaded.

The stitches are different lengths

Check whether the needle is blunt or unsuitable for the fabric and that it is inserted correctly. (Test this on a scrap of fabric before beginning the project.) Try stitching with the needle in the left or right position. On fine fabrics, put tissue paper under the presser foot.

The top thread keeps breaking

Manufacturers recommend that you change needles every time you change the type of thread. This is because each thread wears a unique groove in the needle as it is being stitched. Label your needle packet to indicate what type of thread to use with each needle. This is particularly important when doing machine embroidery. Check also that you are using the correct thread and type of needle for the fabric. A knot or slub in the thread or an over-tight top tension can also cause the thread to break.

above A well maintained sewing machine is an indispensable tool for making soft furnishings.

The bobbin thread breaks

Check that the bobbin case is inserted correctly, has not been over-filled, and that the thread has no knots in it. Also check the bobbin case mechanism for trapped fluff (lint). Occasionally, the spring on the bobbin case is too tight for the thread and the tension screw needs to be loosened – refer to your manual for instructions.

choosing fabric

If one of your soft furnishing projects isn't successful, it could be your choice of fabric or the way you handled it that lets it down. With such a wonderful range of fabrics on the market, there is no need for "hand-made" to mean a cheaper alternative or second-best. Staff in most fabric shops will be pleased to pass on their knowledge about choosing the best fabric for a particular purpose.

PREPARING FABRIC

Once you have chosen the fabric, the temptation is to start cutting straight away. Curb your enthusiasm, however – a little time spent preparing the fabric before you begin will help prevent costly mistakes later.

Before beginning any soft furnishing project, the first thing to do is to straighten the fabric. When fabric is wrapped around a large bolt or roll, it can be pulled slightly out of shape and this may not become obvious until you have already started sewing. Problems such as the pattern not matching, cushion covers that aren't square, curtains not hanging straight, or a swag draping incorrectly can all be caused by the fabric being slightly off-grain.

To check whether the fabric is straight or off-grain, first straighten the ends, either by tearing the fabric or by pulling a thread (see below), then fold it in half lengthways with the selvages together to see if the two crossways ends meet squarely. Sometimes it isn't obvious that the fabric is not straight because the bolt was used as a guide for cutting in the store, which can make the end look straight. Always check it anyway – it will help to ensure perfect results.

left Always choose fabrics that are suitable for the job in hand.

STRAIGHTENING FABRIC ENDS

If the fabric has an obvious weave, or a woven pattern such as a check, it can easily be cut along the grain to ensure it is straight. In most cases, however, you will have to tear or cut along a thread to guarantee a straight line.

Tearing is the quickest way to straighten a fabric end but this is only suitable for plain-weave fabrics such as calico or poplin. Try a test piece first to ensure that tearing the fabric won't harm it, or cause it to tear lengthways. The safest way to straighten the end is by pulling a thread. This takes longer, but is worth it.

1 Look carefully at the weave of the fabric and snip into the selvage next to where the first thread goes straight across. Pull one of the crossways threads until the fabric gathers up.

2 Ease the gathers gently along the thread as far as possible, then cut carefully along this line. Continue this process until you have cut right across the fabric.

STRAIGHTENING THE GRAIN

Once the end of the fabric is straight, you will be able to check if the fabric is off-grain. There are two ways to do this. You can either lay the fabric flat on a square table or fold it in half lengthways with the selvages together. In both cases, the ends should be square. If the corners don't match, the fabric needs to be straightened before you

can begin cutting and sewing. If it is only slightly off-grain it can be steam-pressed into shape, but misshapen fabric must be pulled back into shape. This can be quite hard work for a large piece of fabric, and you may need to enlist the help of a friend to pull from the opposite end. This step is essential and will affect the final drape of the fabric, so don't be tempted to miss this stage.

To pull the fabric back into shape, hold it firmly on each side of the narrow corners and pull your hands apart. Keep moving your hands down each side, pulling firmly until you reach the other corners. This is easier to do if two people work from opposite corners. Fold the fabric in half lengthways, right sides together. Pin the raw edges together. Place pins into the ironing board every 13cm/5in along the selvage. Press the fabric from the selvage into the fold until the weave is absolutely straight, but avoid pressing the fold. Leave the fabric to cool before removing the pins. For pressing large pieces of fabric cover a table with a blanket and sheet.

fabric terminology

It is important to understand the terms used when describing fabric. Some fabrics handle very differently if cut on the crossways grain rather than the lengthways grain, and designs can end up facing in the wrong direction. Most fabrics are cut with the right sides of the fabric together, and can be folded on the lengthways or crossways fold. Nap designs have a design or surface texture, which means that the fabric must be folded lengthways or not at all.

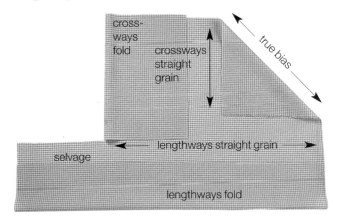

Bias

The bias is any diagonal line across woven fabric. Bias strips are used for binding or piping curved edges. Fabric cut on the bias has more stretch than fabric cut on the straight grain, and the most stretch is achieved on the

true bias; this is when the selvage edge on one side is folded over to run parallel to the crossways grain.

Fold

Fabric is usually sold off a bolt or roll. On narrow widths the fabric is flat with a selvage at each edge, but on wider widths the fabric is folded in half lengthways so that the selvages lie together. This fold indicates where the centre of a large design or pattern should lie.

Grain

Woven fabrics are made up of two sets of threads. The crossways, or weft, threads go over and under the stronger warp threads which run the length of the fabric. The grain is the direction in which these threads have been woven. Warp threads running parallel to the selvage are on the lengthways grain. When the weft threads run perpendicular to the selvage, they are on the crossways grain.

Selvage

This is the narrow, flat band running lengthways down each side of the fabric. Here the threads are strong and closely woven, and provide a straight, ready-finished edge for seams such as the zipper opening in a cushion cover or sheer curtains.

patterned fabrics

Many soft furnishing fabrics have a pattern or design, including checks and stripes. For large-scale projects such as covering an armchair, extra fabric is usually required to accommodate the design. It is always a good idea to make a pattern in cheap calico or lining fabric for any three-dimensional project, before cutting out.

There are various rules, most of which are a matter of common sense. For example, when working on a slip cover for an armchair or sofa, you can mark the centre of the seat inside back and the centre of the seat cushion on the calico pattern before laying it on the fabric. Patterned curtains and pelmets have their own rules. In general, position a complete repeat of the design along the hem and ignore part-repeats along the top edge. On pelmets choose the shape carefully to accommodate the pattern on the fabric.

MATCHING PATTERN REPEATS

Patterned fabrics are generally repeated down the length of the fabric, either as a normal or "drop" repeat. The fabric should be marked with its repeat length when you buy it, and sometimes it is much larger than it appears. Fabrics such as *toile de jouy* have large motifs that are printed in a drop repeat. These can sometimes be matched more easily on the half-width, which is useful when making curtains.

Cut the centre panel of any piece of soft furnishing fabric to the correct length, then position the next length so that the pattern matches across the width. Cut off the excess fabric.

above *Use large dressmaking scissors to cut.*

WORKING WITH STRIPES AND CHECKS

It can be a challenge working with stripes and checks for soft furnishing, though you can choose carefully to suit the project. For example, the Roman blind in this book has vertical rather than horizontal stripes because these caused no problems for cutting or making up. The following are a few tricks of the trade, useful when working with striped and checked fabric.

1 On a project such as a cushion cover, back the striped or checked fabric with a plain fabric that picks out one of the colours, instead of trying to match the pattern exactly.

2 Where one stripe overlaps or joins another (e.g. on a flap cushion, the valance on a slipcover, or a pelmet and curtain), alternate the direction of the stripes.

MATCHING STRIPES AND CHECKS

The pattern repeat on check fabrics is more distinct and not as large as other fabrics, but the seams are more of a challenge to match. In some cases it is sufficient to match the pattern horizontally only, but with the large expanses of fabric used in soft furnishing it is essential to match vertically as well. The following method can be used for all striped, checked and patterned fabrics. It ensures that the pattern continues across a curtain or tablecloth, matching exactly at the seam.

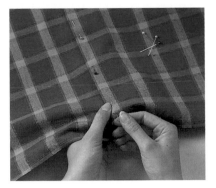

1 Cut the centre panel, then match the fabric horizontally down the seams. Cut off the excess fabric.

2 Turn over and press the seam allowance on one edge. Pin the folded edge to the next length of fabric, matching the pattern horizontally and vertically.

3 Slip-tack (baste) the seam from the right side by slipping the needle along the fold, then taking a similar-size stitch through the other fabric. The seam can then be stitched as normal.

USING PATTERNS FOR EFFECT

Soft furnishings can be very striking when the pattern or stripe is used to accentuate a decorative feature. Avoid problems by choosing the fabric carefully.

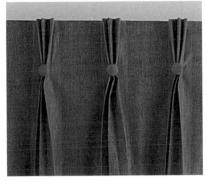

1 Hand-stitched triple pleats work perfectly with this vertically striped fabric. The spacing of the pleats can be adjusted to suit the width and spacing of the stripes.

2 Triple pleat tape on the other hand pulls the fabric up so that a different stripe pattern appears on each group of pleats. A pencil pleat tape would be a better choice.

3 London blinds have a deep box pleat either side that opens as the blind is pulled up. The pansy pattern on this striped fabric has been placed in the centre of the pleats to accentuate this feature.

USING NAP FABRIC

Nap fabrics are fabrics that can only be cut and hung in one direction. If the fabric has a one-way design, it is obvious which way it has to be cut. Pattern pieces for pile fabrics, such as corduroy or velvet, must be cut facing the same direction. These fabrics catch the light in a certain way and look much darker when the pile is facing up and lighter when facing down.

right *The direction of the nap can be determined by running your hand over the surface.*

making seams

Various seams are used in different soft furnishing projects, depending on whether the finished item needs to be strong, to withstand frequent washing or to be purely decorative.

FLAT SEAM

This is the basic seam used in most soft furnishing projects. The size of the seam allowance varies, but is usually 1.5cm/⅝in. Even if the seam will be trimmed, stitch a wider seam and trim it to get a stronger join.

1 Pin the two layers of fabric together, matching the raw edges carefully.

2 Tack (baste) 1.5cm/⅝ in in from the edge. If the fabric is fairly firm, it is possible to stitch across the pins without the need for tacking.

3 Stitch along one side of the tacking thread. Press the seam open. Zigzag-stitch or overcast the edges to prevent fraying.

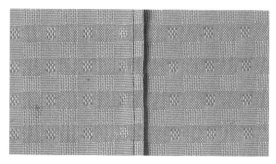

FRENCH SEAM

A French seam is suitable for lightweight fabrics. It is used on bed linen to make strong seams that will not fray. The finished width of the seam can be narrower on fine fabrics.

1 Wrong sides together, stitch a 7mm/⅜in seam. Trim to 3mm/⅛ in.

2 Press the seam open. This makes it much easier to get the fold exactly on the edge at the next stage.

3 Fold, enclosing the raw edges, and press. Pin the seam and stitch 5mm/¼ in from the edge. Press to one side.

LAPPED SEAM

This seam is ideal for joining fabric that requires accurate matching as it is stitched from the right side. Plan carefully when cutting out pattern pieces in order to make the seam as inconspicuous as possible.

1 Turn under 1cm/½ in along a straight thread and press.

2 Lay the pressed edge on top of the other piece of fabric. Pin along the fold, carefully matching the design.

3 Tack (baste) the fabric if it is slippery, otherwise stitch carefully over the pins, close to the fold. For extra strength and decoration, top-stitch a further row 5mm/¼ in away.

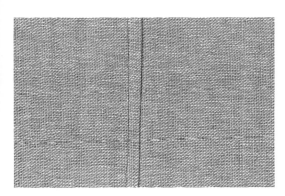

FLAT FELL SEAM

This is the traditional seam used for denim jeans. It is a strong seam that can be washed and wears well, as all the raw edges are enclosed. It is most suitable for mediumweight fabrics.

1 Pin the fabric right sides together and stitch a plain 1.5cm/⅝in seam. (For the traditional finish with two rows of stitching showing, begin with the fabric wrong sides together instead.)

2 Trim one side of the seam allowance to 3mm/⅛in. Press the wide seam allowance over the trimmed edge.

3 Turn under the edge of the larger seam allowance and pin then tack. Stitch close to the edge of the fold.

ENCLOSED SEAMS

Seams that are enclosed (for example, inside a cushion cover) do not need to be finished, but in order to achieve a neat line when the cover is turned through they should be trimmed carefully. Bulky seams should be layered. Curved seams and corners need to be trimmed, and also snipped or notched into the seam allowance.

1 Stitch around a curved edge, using the lines on the needle plate as a guide for stitching. When you get to the corner, leave the needle in the fabric and rotate the fabric until the next seam is lined up.

2 Snip into any inward-facing points or curves to within one or two threads of the stitching. Trim the seam allowance to 5mm/¼in.

3 Cut across any outward-facing points. If the fabric is medium- or heavyweight, trim the seam allowance on either side slightly as well.

4 Notch the outward-facing curves. Cut notches closer together on tight curves, and every 2.5–5cm/1 2in on shallow curves.

5 If the seams have been stitched with multiple layers of fabric, trim them to reduce bulk. Grade the seam allowances so that the edge that is next to the right side is the largest.

mitring corners

Mitring is the neatest way to finish corners on soft furnishings. The type of mitre used depends on the item and the type of fabric. The majority of curtains use an uneven mitre but sheer curtains use a double mitre. Double mitres are suitable for sheer fabric, or the turned-in hem edge will be visible through the hem.

SINGLE MITRE

Use a single mitre on firm, closely woven fabrics, where the shorter turning inside the hem edge will not show through, even against the light.

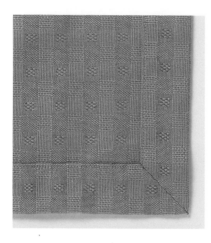

1 Trim the fabric along the straight grain. Turn over and press the hem allowance.

2 Open out the hem and press the corner over on the diagonal, exactly where the folds cross. Trim this flap to 5 mm/¼ in.

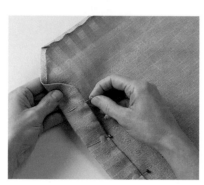

3 ◁ Press a 5mm/¼ in turning along the edge of the hem, including along the diagonal line. Fold the hem over and pin in place. Tack (baste) then stitch along the inner edge of the hem.

4 ▷ Slip-stitch the diagonal seam of the mitre closed as shown.

UNEVEN MITRE

The uneven mitre is used almost exclusively for curtain hems. The fabric isn't trimmed before folding. The extra weight helps the curtain to hang straight.

1 Fold and press a 2cm/¾in double hem down each side and a double 8cm/3in hem along the bottom. Pin the point where the bottom hem meets the side hem. Open the hems, pin 4cm/1½ in from the edge.

2 Fold over the corner between the pins diagonally and press flat.

3 Refold the side and bottom hems to make a neat uneven mitre and pin. Slip stitch the mitre.

DOUBLE MITRE

Use a double mitre on sheer or lightweight fabrics, and on the edge of flat curtains or blinds where the light will shine through the fabric.

1 Trim the fabric along the straight grain. Fold and press a double hem on each edge of the fabric.

2 Open out the double hem and fold the corner over on the diagonal, exactly where the outside folds cross. Trim this flap to 5mm/¼in.

3 Refold the double hem and pin the mitred corner neatly. If the diagonal raw edge is showing, open up the corner and trim. Finish as for the single mitre.

RAW EDGE MITRE

This basic mitre is used if the back of the fabric will be lined. The lining is slip-stitched into position in the middle of the hem to cover the raw edges.

1 Trim the fabric along the straight grain. Fold and press the hem allowance, then open out.

2 Press the corner over diagonally, exactly on the pressed crease. Refold the hem and pin. Slip-stitch the mitre.

right *Mitres can be used as an integral part of the project design. This curtain makes good use of a fabric that is attractive on both sides.*

turning hems

A hem is the most common way to finish the side and bottom edges of soft furnishings. Machine-stitched hems are usually quite acceptable on simple unlined curtains and modern slipcovers, but more elaborate fabrics and curtains in a more formal style should really be hand stitched.

Hems can be either single or double. A single hem has a single layer of fabric, with the raw edge turned under or finished by zigzag stitch or overcasting. A double hem has a double turning, with the raw edge lying inside along the bottom fold. It is used when the fabric is translucent, or to add weight to a curtain.

MACHINE-STITCHED HEM

This is usually narrower for side hems and deeper for a bottom hem. It is used mainly with light- and mediumweight cotton or linen fabrics. Fold and pin a single or double hem depending on the type of fabric. Stitch along the edge of the fold from the reverse side.

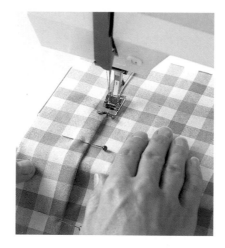
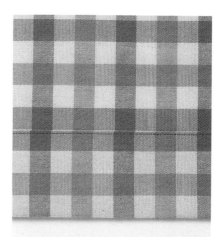

MACHINE-ROLLED HEM

This is used to finish the edge of sheer or lightweight fabrics. Fold a narrow 1cm/½in single hem and stitch along the fold. Trim close to the stitching, fold again then stitch on top of the previous stitching.

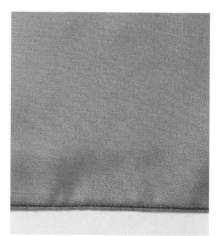

MACHINE BLIND HEMMING

This is quick and easy once you have adjusted the needle position. Tack (baste) the hem 5mm/¼in from the upper fold. Fit the special foot into the machine and fold the hem back under the main fabric along the tacked line. Select the blind hemming stitch and take a few stitches. Alter the width of the needle swing so that you catch only one or two threads of the main fabric.

HERRINGBONE STITCH

Herringbone stitch is a stable hemming stitch usually worked on lined and interlined curtains, especially if the fabric is quite thick. Beginning at the left, take a back stitch into the hem and then further to the right take another back stitch into the main fabric or interlining. Work from right to left if you are left-handed.

HAND HEMMING

This tends to produce a ridge on the right side of the fabric, so it is most often used to stitch bindings or facings in place. The stitches are stronger when worked into the stitching on the reverse side. Pick up one or two threads of fabric or a machined stitch then take a small diagonal stitch into the hem.

SLIP HEMMING

This hand stitch is one of the most common hem finishes, used on light- and mediumweight fabrics. Work the stitches fairly loosely so that there is no ridge on the right side. Pick up one or two threads of fabric, then slide the needle along inside the hem for 5–15mm/¼-½in.

HAND BLIND HEMMING

This is worked in a similar way to slip hemming, but there is less risk of a ridge on the right side as the stitching is worked between the layers of fabric. Tack (baste) 5mm/¼in from the edge of the hem. Fold the edge of the hem over and hold with your thumb. Pick up one or two threads of fabric and then take one or two stitches into the hem.

hand stitching

The majority of soft furnishings are stitched by machine, but there is often also a need for some temporary or permanent hand stitching. Temporary stitches such as tacking (basting) are used to hold fabric in position before stitching and are usually removed later. Permanent stitches include hemming and hidden stitches such as lock stitch, which is used to support curtain linings and interlinings.

TACKING (BASTING)

Work small, even tacking (basting) stitches along seams to secure before stitching. Longer, uneven tacking stitches are used to stitch substantial distances, for example, when temporarily stitching a lining before lock stitching.

SLIP TACKING (BASTING)

This is worked from the right side of the fabric. Turn over and press one seam allowance. Match the pattern along the seam and pin. Work small, even tacking (basting) stitches alternatively along the fold and then into the fabric.

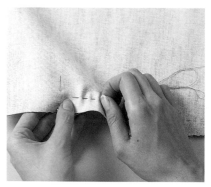

RUNNING STITCH

This stitch is so called because several stitches are "run" along the needle at one time. Keep the spaces and stitches the same size. It is used for awkward seams where there is no strain.

BACK STITCH

This strong stitch is used to complete seams that would be difficult to reach by machine. Half back stitch is similar but stronger – work it in the same way as back stitch, but taking a small stitch only halfway back to the previous stitch.

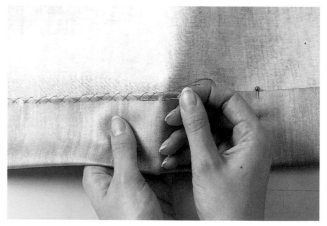

HERRINGBONE STITCH

This is often thought of as an embroidery stitch but it is also useful in soft furnishings. It can be worked in small stitches instead of hemming, or as much larger stitches to hold layers of fabric together when making curtains.

templates

Enlarge the templates to the required size by enlarging them on a photocopier. Alternatively, place a grid over the templates and on a larger grid plot the points where the template crosses the grid line. Join up the dots to make a complete shape.

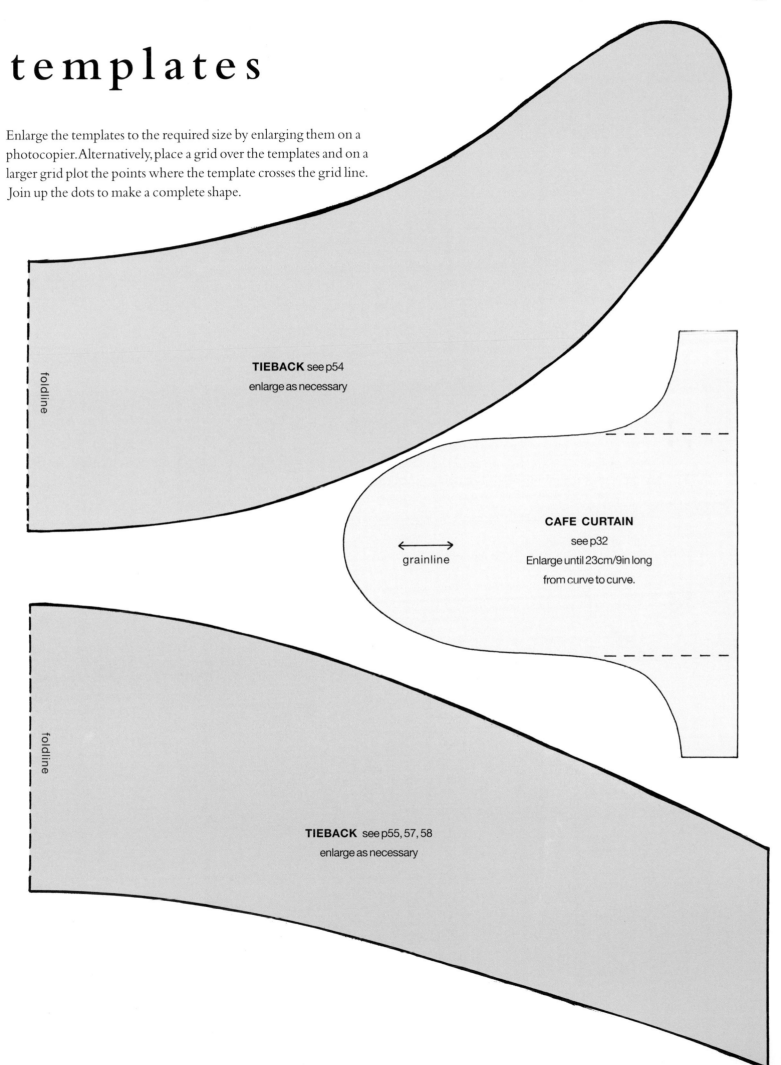

foldline

TIEBACK see p54

enlarge as necessary

grainline

CAFE CURTAIN

see p32

Enlarge until 23cm/9in long

from curve to curve.

foldline

TIEBACK see p55, 57, 58

enlarge as necessary

index